Standards Practice Book

For Home or School

Grade K

Houghton Mifflin Harcourt

INCLUDES:

- Home or School Practice
- Lesson Practice and Test Preparation
- English and Spanish School-Home Letters
- Getting Ready for Grade 1 Lessons

Printed in the U.S.A.

ISBN 978-0-544-23088-0

15 16 17 18 19 20 0928 22 21

4500821043   B C D E F G

 # Number and Operations

COMMON CORE **Critical Area** Representing, relating, and operating on whole numbers, initially with sets of objects

1 Represent, Count, and Write Numbers 0 to 5

Domain Counting and Cardinality
Common Core Standards K.CC.3, K.CC.4a, K.CC.4b, K.CC.4c

2 Compare Numbers to 5

Domain Counting and Cardinality
Common Core Standard K.CC.6

3 | Represent, Count, and Write Numbers 6 to 9

Domain Counting and Cardinality
Common Core Standards K.CC.3, K.CC.5, K.CC.6

4 | Represent and Compare Numbers to 10

Domains Counting and Cardinality
Operations and Algebraic Thinking
Common Core Standards K.CC.2, K.CC.3, K.CC.5, K.CC.6, K.CC.7, K.OA.4

5 Addition

Domain Operations and Algebraic Thinking
Common Core Standards K.OA.1, K.OA.2, K.OA.3, K.OA.5

6 Subtraction

Domain Operations and Algebraic Thinking
Common Core Standards K.OA.1, K.OA.2, K.OA.5

7 Represent, Count, and Write 11 to 19

Domains Counting and Cardinality
Number and Operations in Base Ten
Common Core Standards K.CC.3, K.NBT.1

8 Represent, Count, and Write 20 and Beyond

Domain Counting and Cardinality
Common Core Standards K.CC.1, K.CC.2, K.CC.3, K.CC.5, K.CC.6

 **Geometry and Positions**

 COMMON CORE **Critical Area** Describing shapes and space

9 Identify and Describe Two-Dimensional Shapes

Domain Geometry
Common Core Standards K.G.2, K.G.4, K.G.6

10 Identify and Describe Three-Dimensional Shapes

Domain Geometry
Common Core Standards K.G.1, K.G.2, K.G.3, K.G.4, K.G.5

 **Measurement and Data**

CRITICAL AREA

COMMON CORE | **Critical Area** Representing, relating, and operating on whole numbers, initially with sets of objects

11 Measurement

Domain Measurement and Data
Common Core Standards K.MD.1, K.MD.2

12 Classify and Sort Data

Domain Measurement and Data
Common Core Standard K.MD.3

End-of-Year Resources

Getting Ready for Grade 1

These lessons review important skills and prepare you for Grade 1.

School-Home **Letter**

Dear Family,

My class started Chapter 1 this week. In this chapter, I will show, count, and write numbers 0 to 5.

Love, _____

Vocabulary

one a number for a single object

two one more than one

Home Activity

Use this five frame and counters, such as buttons. Have your child place counters in the five frame to show the numbers 0 to 5. For 0, have your child place one counter in the five frame, and then remove it. Together, practice writing the numbers 0 to 5.

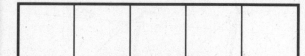

Literature

Look for this book in a library. This book will reinforce your child's counting skills.

Fish Eyes: A Book You Can Count On
by Lois Ehlert.
Voyager Books, 1992.

Carta
para la casa

Querida familia:

Mi clase comenzó el Capítulo 1 esta semana. En este capítulo mostraré, contaré y escribiré números del 0 al 5.

Con cariño, _____

Vocabulario

uno el número de un solo objeto

dos uno más que uno

Actividad para la casa

Use este cuadro de cinco y fichas, tales como botones. Pídale a su hijo que ponga las fichas en el cuadro para mostrar los números del 0 al 5. Para 0, pídale que coloque una ficha en el cuadro de cinco y luego que la quite. Juntos, practiquen la escritura de los números del 0 al 5.

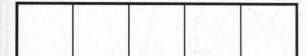

Literatura

Busque este libro en una biblioteca. Este libro ayudarán a su hijo a reforzar la destreza de contar.

Fish Eyes: A Book You Can Count On por Lois Ehlert. Voyager Books, 1992.

Name _____

Model and Count 1 and 2

COMMON CORE STANDARD—K.CC.4A
Count to tell the number of objects.

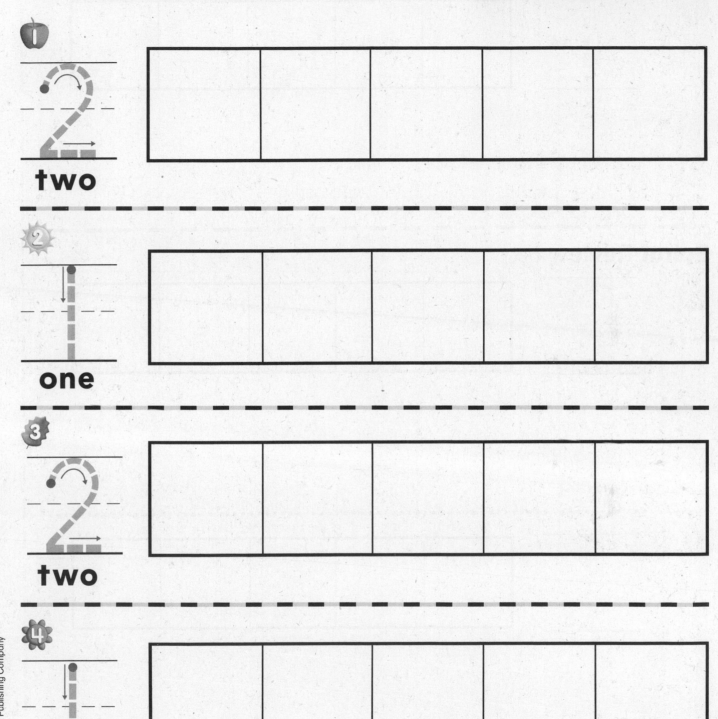

1 🍎

2
two

2 ☀️

1
one

3 🍂

2
two

4 ✿

1
one

DIRECTIONS 1–4. Say the number. Count out that many counters in the five frame. Draw the counters.

Lesson Check <small>(K.CC.4a)</small>

 1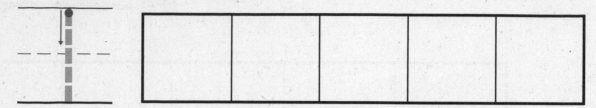

Spiral Review <small>(K.CC.4a)</small>

2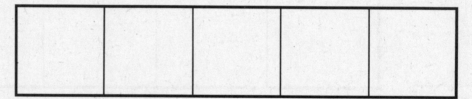

3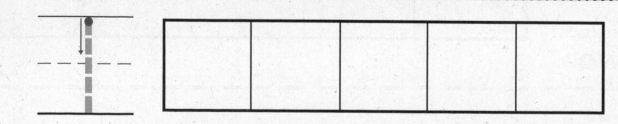

DIRECTIONS 1–3. Trace the number. How many counters would you place in the five frame to show the number? Draw the counters.

Count and Write 1 and 2

COMMON CORE STANDARD—K.CC.3
Know number names and the count sequence.

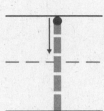

DIRECTIONS 1–4. Count and tell how many. Write the number.

Lesson Check (K.CC.3)

_____
- - - - - - - -
_____

Spiral Review (K.CC.4a)

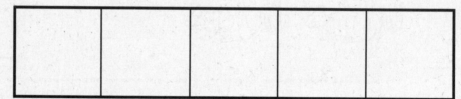

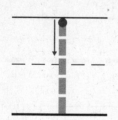

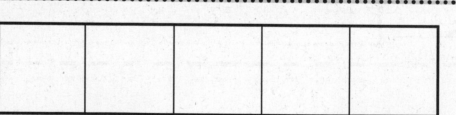

DIRECTIONS 1. Count and tell how many cubes. Write the number.
2–3. Trace the number. How many counters would you place in the five frame to show the number? Draw the counters.

Model and Count 3 and 4

COMMON CORE STANDARD—K.CC.4A
Count to tell the number of objects.

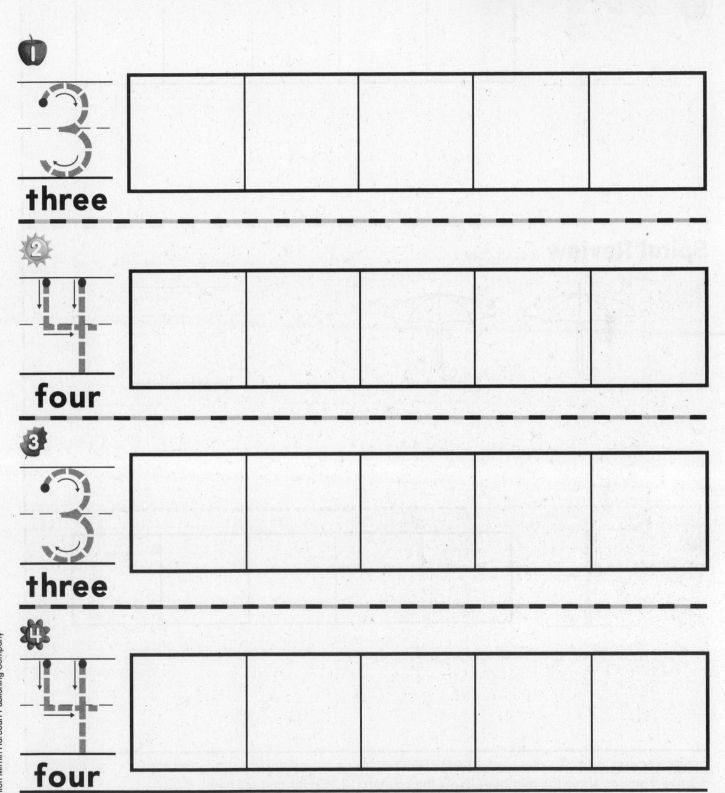

1 3 three

2 4 four

3 3 three

4 4 four

DIRECTIONS 1–4. Say the number as you trace it. Count out that many counters in the five frame. Draw the counters.

Lesson Check (K.CC.4a)

Spiral Review (K.CC.3, K.CC.4a)

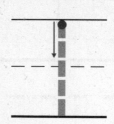 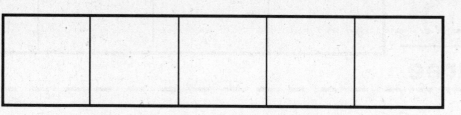

DIRECTIONS 1. Trace the number. How many counters would you place in the five frame to show the number? Draw the counters. 2. Count and tell how many umbrellas. Write the number. 3. Trace the number. How many counters would you place in the five frame to show the number? Draw the counters.

Name _____

Count and Write 3 and 4

COMMON CORE STANDARD—K.CC.3
Know number names and the count sequence.

 1

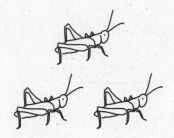 

 2

 _____

_ _ _ _ _ _ _ _ _ _ _

_____

3

 _____

_ _ _ _ _ _ _ _ _ _ _

_____

 4

 _____

_ _ _ _ _ _ _ _ _ _ _

_____

5

 _____

_ _ _ _ _ _ _ _ _ _ _

_____

6

 _____

_ _ _ _ _ _ _ _ _ _ _

_____

DIRECTIONS 1–6. Count and tell how many. Write the number.

Chapter 1

© Houghton Mifflin Harcourt Publishing Company

Lesson Check (K.CC.3)

 1

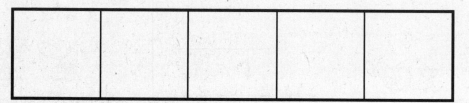

_____

- - - - - -

_____

Spiral Review (K.CC.3, K.CC.4a)

 2

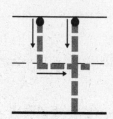

 3

_____

- - - - - -

_____

DIRECTIONS 1. Count and tell how many butterflies. Write the number.
2. Trace the number. How many counters would you place in the five frame
to show the number? Draw the counters. 3. Count and tell how many
flowers. Write the number.

Model and Count 5

COMMON CORE STANDARD—K.CC.4A
Count to tell the number of objects.

1

2

3

4

DIRECTIONS 1. Place counters to show five. Draw the counters. Write the number. 2. Place counters to show three. Draw the counters. Write the number. 3. Place counters to show four. Draw the counters. Write the number. 4. Place counters to show five. Draw the counters. Write the number.

Lesson Check (K.CC.4a)

 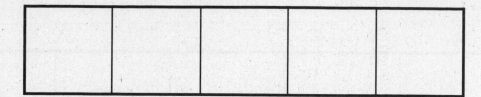

Spiral Review (K.CC.3)

_____

- - - - - - - - - - - -

_____

_____

- - - - - - - - - - - -

_____

DIRECTIONS 1. Trace the number. How many counters would you place in the five frame to show the number? Draw the counters.
2–3. Count and tell how many. Write the number.

Name _____

Count and Write to 5

COMMON CORE STANDARDS—K.CC.4B
Count to tell the number of objects.

1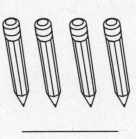

_____

- - - - - - -

_____

2

_____

- - - - - - -

_____

3 ERASER ERASER ERASER

_____

- - - - - - -

_____

4

_____

- - - - - - -

_____

5

_____

- - - - - - -

_____

6

_____

- - - - - - -

_____

DIRECTIONS 1–6. Count and tell how many. Write the number.

Lesson Check (K.CC.4b)

_____

- - - - - - - -

_____

Spiral Review (K.CC.3, K.CC.4a)

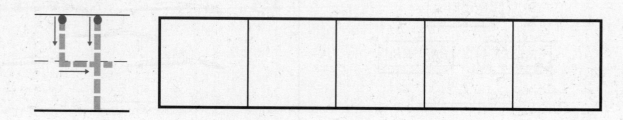

_____

- - - - - - - -

_____

DIRECTIONS 1. Count and tell how many animals. Write the number. 2. Trace the number. How many counters would you place in the five frame to show the number? Draw the counters. 3. Count and tell how many cubes. Write the number.

Name _____

Algebra • Ways to Make 5

COMMON CORE STANDARD—K.CC.4B
Understand addition as putting together and adding to, and understand subtraction as taking apart and taking from.

1

_ _ _ _ _ _ _   ◯   **and**   _ _ _ _ _ _ _   ◯

2

_ _ _ _ _ _ _   ◯   **and**   _ _ _ _ _ _ _   ◯

DIRECTIONS 1–2. Use two colors of counters to show a way to make 5. Color to show the counters. Write the numbers to show the pair that makes 5.

Chapter 1

Lesson Check (K.OA.3)

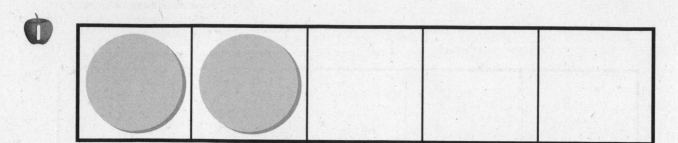

  2

2 **and** ------ **more**

Spiral Review (K.CC.3, K.CC.4b)

_____
- - - - - - -
_____

_____
- - - - - - -
_____

DIRECTIONS 1. How many more counters would you place in the five frame to show a way to make 5? Draw the counters. Write the number. **2–3.** Count and tell how many. Write the number.

Name _____

Count and Order to 5

COMMON CORE STANDARD—K.CC.4C
Count to tell the number of objects.

1

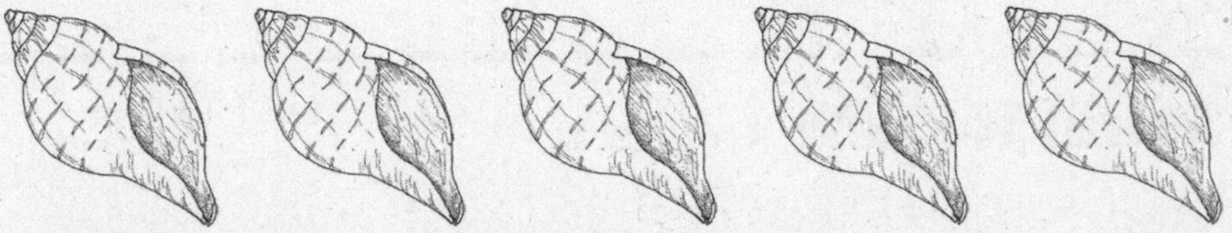

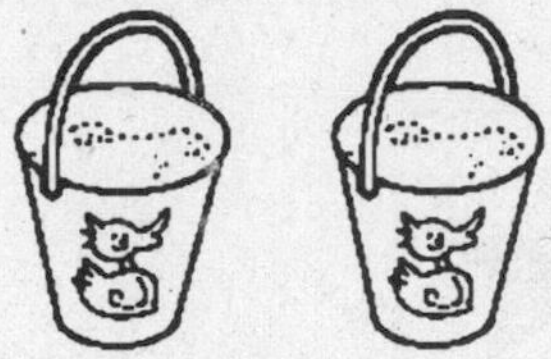

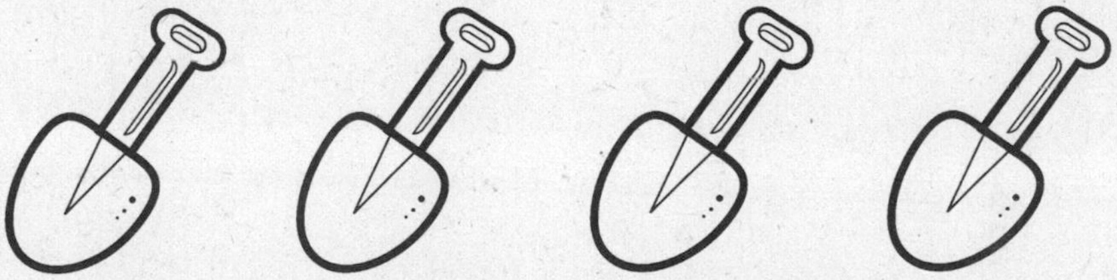

DIRECTIONS **1.** Count the objects in each set. Write the number beside the set of objects. Write those numbers in order beginning with number 1.

Lesson Check

1, 2, 3, _____, 5

Spiral Review (K.CC.3c, K.CC.4a)

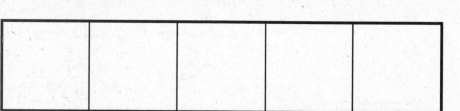

DIRECTIONS **1.** Write the numbers in order. **2.** Count and tell how many stars. Write the number. **3.** Trace the number. How many counters would you place in the five frame to show the number? Draw the counters.

Problem Solving • Understand 0

COMMON CORE STANDARD—K.CC.3
Know number names and the count sequence.

_____

- - - - - - -

_____

_____

- - - - - - -

_____

DIRECTIONS Use counters to model these problems. **1.** Oliver has one juice box. Lucy has one fewer juice box than Oliver. How many juice boxes does Lucy have? Write the number. **2.** Jessica has no books. Wesley has 2 more books than Jessica. How many books does Wesley have? Write the number.

Chapter 1

Lesson Check (K.CC.3)

_____

- - - - - - -

_____

Spiral Review (K.CC.3)

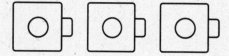

_____

- - - - - - -

_____

_____

- - - - - - -

_____

DIRECTIONS 1. Use counters to model this problem. Eva has 2 apples in her basket. She eats 1 apple and gives 1 apple to her friend. How many apples does Eva have now? Write the number. **2–3.** Count and tell how many. Write the number.

Identify and Write 0

COMMON CORE STANDARDS—K.CC.3
Know number names and the count sequence.

 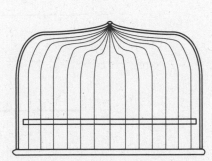

 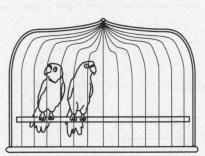

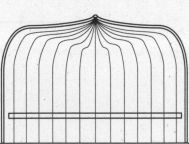 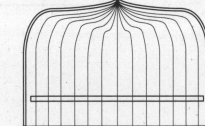 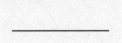

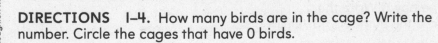

DIRECTIONS   1–4. How many birds are in the cage? Write the
number. Circle the cages that have 0 birds.

Lesson Check (K.CC.3)

_____

- - - - - - - - -

_____

Spiral Review (K.CC.4a, K.CC.4b)

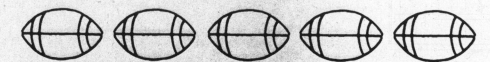

_____

- - - - - - - - -

_____

3

_____

- - - - - - - - -

_____

DIRECTIONS **1.** How many fish are in the bowl? Write the number.   **2.** Count and tell how many. Write the number.   **3.** Draw a set of 5 marbles. Write the number.

School-Home Letter

Dear Family,

My class started Chapter 2 this week. In this chapter, I will learn how to build and compare sets to help me compare numbers.

Love, _____

Vocabulary

same number

○ ○
△ △

There are the same number of circles and triangles.

greater

○ ○ ○
△ △

The number of circles is greater than the number of triangles.

less

○ ○
△ △ △

The number of circles is less than the number of triangles.

Home Activity

Gather two sets of five household items. Line some of them up on a table in two groups of different quantities. Ask your child to count and tell you how many are in each set. Have your child point to the set that has the greater number of objects. Then ask your child to point to the set with the number of objects that is less.

Change the number in each group and repeat the activity.

Literature

Look for this book in the library. It will help reinforce concepts of comparing.

More, Fewer, Less by Tana Hoban. Greenwillow Books, 1998.

Carta para la casa

Querida familia:

Mi clase comenzó el Capítulo 2 esta semana. En este capítulo, aprenderé cómo construir y comparar conjuntos que me ayuden a comparar números.

Con cariño, _____

Vocabulario

igual número

○ ○
△ △

Hay igual número de círculos y triángulos.

mayor

○ ○ ○
△ △

El número de círculos es mayor que el número de triángulos.

menor

○ ○
△ △ △

El número de círculos es menor que el número de triángulos.

Actividad para la casa

Reúna dos conjuntos con cinco elementos de la casa. Alinee sobre la mesa algunos de ellos en dos grupos de diferentes cantidades. Pídale a su hijo que cuente y diga cuántos hay en cada conjunto. Dígale que señale el conjunto que tiene el mayor número de objetos. Luego, pídale que señale el conjunto con el menor número de objetos.

Cambie el número en cada grupo y repita la actividad.

Literatura

Busque este libro en la biblioteca. Este libro ayudará a su hijo a reforzar los conceptos de más y menos.

More, Fewer, Less
por Tana Hoban.
Greenwillow Books, 1998.

Same Number

COMMON CORE STANDARD—K.CC.6
Compare numbers.

_____

- - - - - - - -

_____

_____

- - - - - - - -

_____

DIRECTIONS 1. Compare the sets of objects. Is the number of dolphins greater than, less than, or the same as the number of turtles? Count how many dolphins. Write the number. Count how many turtles. Write the number. Tell a friend what you know about the number of objects in each set.

Lesson Check (K.CC.6)

_____

- - - - - - - -

_____

- - - - - - - -

_____

Spiral Review (K.CC.3, K.CC.4a)

_____

- - - - - - - -

_____

 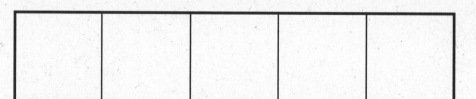

DIRECTIONS 1. Count how many cars. Write the number. Draw to show a set of counters that has the same number as the set of cars. Write the number. Draw lines to match the objects in each set. **2.** Count and tell how many birds are in the cage. Write the number. **3.** Trace the number. How many counters would you place in the five frame to show the number? Draw the counters.

Greater Than

COMMON CORE STANDARD—K.CC.6
Compare numbers.

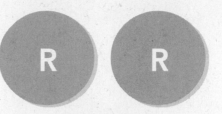

_____   _____

- - - - -   - - - - -

_____   _____

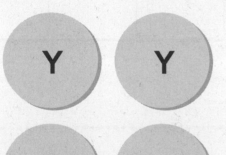

_____   _____

- - - - -   - - - - -

_____   _____

DIRECTIONS   1–2. Place counters as shown. Y is for yellow, and
R is for red. Count and tell how many are in each set. Write the
numbers. Compare the numbers. Circle the number that is greater.

© Houghton Mifflin Harcourt Publishing Company

Lesson Check (K.CC.6)

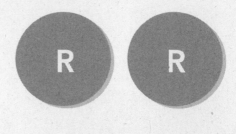

_____   _____

- - - - - - - - -   - - - - - - - - -

_____   _____

Spiral Review (K.CC.4a)

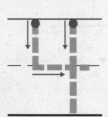

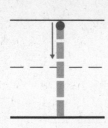

DIRECTIONS 1. Place counters as shown. Y is for yellow, and R is for red. Count and tell how many are in each set. Write the numbers. Compare the numbers. Circle the number that is greater. **2–3.** Trace the number. How many counters would you place in the five frame to show the number? Draw the counters.

Name _____

Less Than

COMMON CORE STANDARD—K.CC.6
Compare numbers.

_____   _____

_ _ _ _ _   _ _ _ _ _

_____   _____

_____   _____

_ _ _ _ _   _ _ _ _ _

_____   _____

DIRECTIONS   I–2. Count and tell how many are in each set. Write the numbers. Compare the numbers. Circle the number that is less.

Lesson Check (K.CC.6)

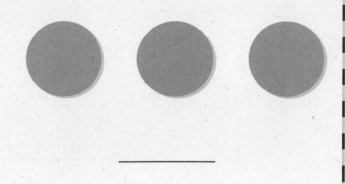

_____   _____

- - - - -   - - - - -

_____   _____

Spiral Review (K.CC.4a, K.CC.4b)

_____

- - - - -

_____

DIRECTIONS **1.** Count and tell how many are in each set. Write the numbers. Compare the numbers. Circle the number that is less. **2.** Trace the number. How many counters would you place in the five frame to show the number? Draw the counters. **3.** Count how many birds. Write the number.

Problem Solving • Compare by Matching Sets to 5

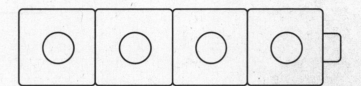

COMMON CORE STANDARD—K.CC.6
Compare numbers.

_____

– – – – – – – – –

_____

– –

2

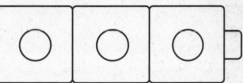

_____

– – – – – – – – –

_____

_____

– – – – – – – – –

_____

DIRECTIONS 1. How many cubes are there? Write the number. Model a cube train that has a number of cubes greater than 4. Draw the cube train. Write how many. Compare the cube trains by matching. Tell a friend about the cube trains. **2.** How many cubes are there? Write the number. Model a cube train that has a number of cubes less than 3. Draw the cube train. Write how many. Compare the cube trains by matching. Tell a friend about the cube trains.

Chapter 2

thirty-one **P31**

Lesson Check (K.CC.6)

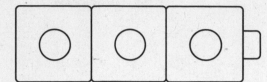

Spiral Review (K.CC.4)

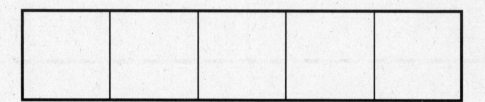

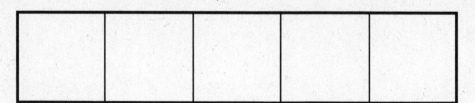

DIRECTIONS I. How many cubes are there? Write the number. Model a cube train that has a number of cubes greater than 3. Draw the cube train. Write how many. Compare the cube trains by matching. Tell a friend about the cube trains. **2–3.** Trace the number. How many counters would you place in the five frame to show the number? Draw the counters.

P32 thirty-two

Name _____

Compare by Counting Sets to 5

 COMMON CORE STANDARD—K.CC.6
Compare numbers.

1

_____

- - - - - - - - - - - - - -

_____

2

_____

- - - - - - - - - - - - - -

_____

3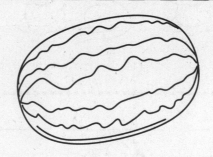

_____

- - - - - - - - - - - - - -

_____

DIRECTIONS 1–2. Count how many objects are in each set.
Write the numbers. Compare the numbers. Circle the number
that is greater. 3. Count how many objects are in each set.
Write the numbers. Compare the numbers. Circle the number
that is less.

Chapter 2

Lesson Check (K.CC.6)

_____

- - - - - - - - - - - -

_____

Spiral Review (K.CC.3, K.CC.4c)

_____

- - - - - - - - - - - -

_____

1, 2, ___, 4, 5

DIRECTIONS 1. Count how many objects are in each set.
Write the numbers. Compare the numbers. Circle the number
that is less. **2.** Count and tell how many cats. Write the number.
3. Write the numbers in order.

Chapter 3

School-Home Letter

Dear Family,

My class started Chapter 3 this week. In this chapter, I will learn how to show, count, and write numbers 6 to 9.

Love, _____

Vocabulary

six one more than five

eight one more than seven

Home Activity

Pour salt or sand into a cookie sheet or baking dish. Pick a number from 6 to 9 and have your child draw the number in the salt or sand. Then ask your child to draw circles to match that number. Shake to erase and begin again!

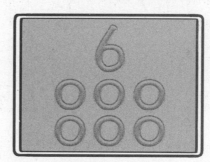

Literature

Look for this book in the library. You and your child will enjoy this fun story that provides reinforcement of counting concepts.

Seven Scary Monsters by Mary Beth Lundgren. Clarion Books, 2003.

Carta para la casa

Querida familia:

Mi clase comenzó el Capítulo 3 esta semana. En este capítulo, aprenderé cómo mostrar, contar y escribir números del 6 al 9.

Con cariño, _____

Vocabulario

seis uno más que cinco

ocho uno más que siete

Actividad para la casa

Ponga sal o arena en una fuente para horno. Elija un número del 6 al 9 y pídale a su hijo que dibuje el número en la sal o la arena. Luego, pídale que dibuje el mismo número de círculos. Mezcle para borrar y ¡comiencen de nuevo!

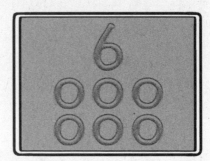

Literatura

Busque este libro en la biblioteca. Usted y su hijo disfrutarán de este cuento divertido que proporciona un refuerzo para los conceptos de contar.

Seven Scary Monsters por Mary Beth Lundgren. Clarion Books, 2003.

Name _____

Model and Count 6

COMMON CORE STANDARD—K.CC.5
Count to tell the number of objects.

six

and

and

and

and

DIRECTIONS 1. Trace the number 6. Use two-color counters to model the different ways to make 6. Color to show the counters below. Write to show some pairs of numbers that make 6.

Chapter 3

Lesson Check (K.CC.5)

 **six**

Spiral Review (K.CC.3, K.CC.6)

DIRECTIONS **1.** Trace the number. How many more counters would you place in the ten frame to model a way to make 6? Draw the counters. **2.** Count and tell how many are in each set. Write the numbers. Compare the numbers. Circle the number that is less. **3.** Count and tell how many. Write the number.

Count and Write to 6

COMMON CORE STANDARD—K.CC.3
Know number names and the count sequence.

1

6
six

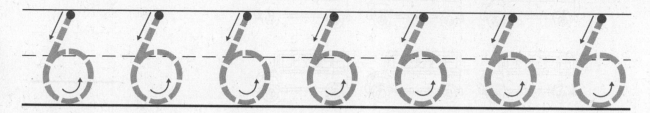

2

_____

- - - - - - - - -

_____

3

_____

- - - - - - - - -

_____

4

_____

- - - - - - - - -

_____

5

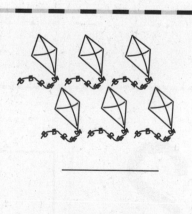

_____

- - - - - - - - -

_____

DIRECTIONS **1.** Say the number. Trace the numbers.
2–5. Count and tell how many. Write the number.

_____

- - - - - - - - - - - - - -

_____

Spiral Review (K.CC.4a, K.CC.6)

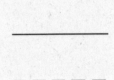

_____

- - - - - - - - - - - - - -

_____

_____

- - - - - - - - - - - - - -

_____

2

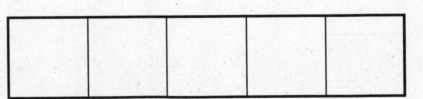

DIRECTIONS **1.** How many school buses are there? Write the number.
2. Count and tell how many are in each set. Write the numbers. Compare the numbers. Circle the number that is greater. **3.** How many counters would you place in the five frame to show the number? Draw the counters.

Name _____

Model and Count 7

COMMON CORE STANDARD—K.CC.5
Count to tell the number of objects.

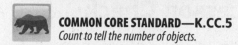

seven

and

and

and

and

DIRECTIONS I. Trace the number 7. Use two-color counters to model the different ways to make 7. Color to show the counters below. Write to show some pairs of numbers that make 7.

Chapter 3

Lesson Check (K.CC.5)

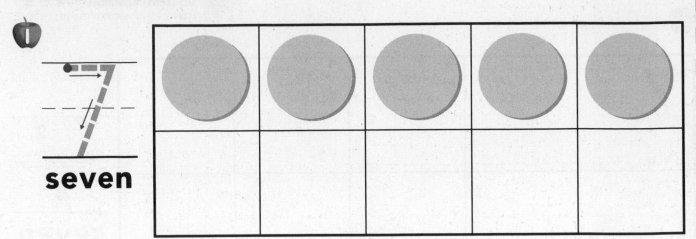

7

seven

Spiral Review (K.CC.3, K.CC.6)

DIRECTIONS **1.** Trace the number. How many more counters would you place in the ten frame to model a way to make 7? Draw the counters. **2.** Count and tell how many are in each set. Write the numbers. Compare the numbers. Circle the number that is less. **3.** Count and tell how many. Write the number.

Count and Write to 7

Lesson 3.4

1

7
seven

7 7 7 7 7 7 7

2

_____

- - - - - - -

_____

3

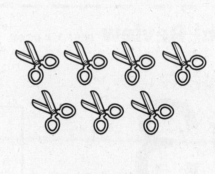

_____

- - - - - - -

_____

4

_____

- - - - - - -

_____

5

_____

- - - - - - -

_____

DIRECTIONS   1. Say the number. Trace the numbers.
2–5. Count and tell how many. Write the number.

Chapter 3

forty-three **P43**

Lesson Check (K.CC.3)

 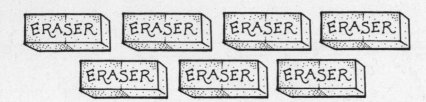

_____

- - - - - - - - - - -

_____

Spiral Review (K.CC.3, K.CC.4a)

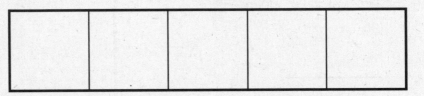

3

_____

- - - - - - - - - - -

_____

DIRECTIONS 1. Count and tell how many erasers. Write the number.
2. How many counters would you place in the five frame to show the number?
Draw the counters. 3. Count and tell how many cubes. Write the number.

Name _____

Model and Count 8

COMMON CORE STANDARD—K.CC.5
Count to tell the number of objects.

1

8
eight

____ ____ and ____ ____

____ ____ and ____ ____

____ ____ and ____ ____

____ ____ and ____ ____

DIRECTIONS 1. Trace the number 8. Use two-color counters to model the different ways to make 8. Color to show the counters below. Write to show some pairs of numbers that make 8.

Chapter 3

Lesson Check (K.CC.5)

1

8
eight

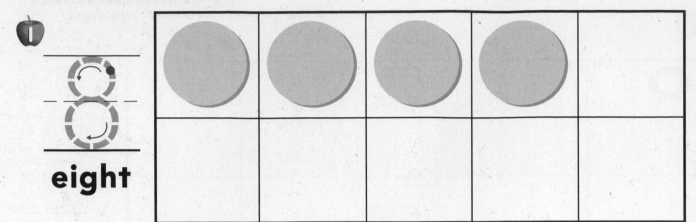

Spiral Review (K.CC.3, K.CC.6)

2

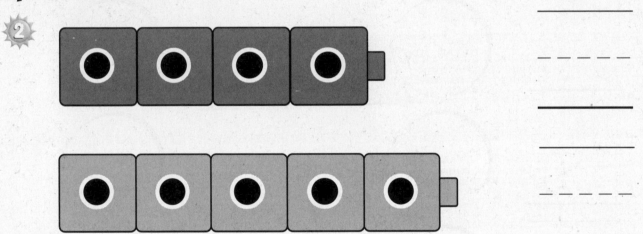

3

DIRECTIONS 1. Trace the number. How many more counters would you place in the ten frame to model a way to make 8? Draw the counters. 2. Count and tell how many are in each set. Write the numbers. Compare the numbers. Circle the number that is greater. 3. Count and tell how many. Write the number.

Count and Write to 8

COMMON CORE STANDARD—K.CC.3
Know number names and the count sequence.

1

8
eight

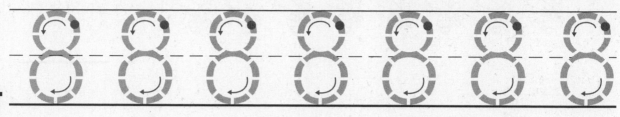

2

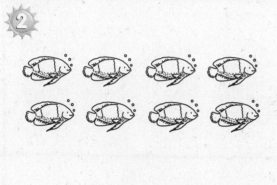

_____

- - - - - - - - -

_____

3

_____

- - - - - - - - -

_____

4

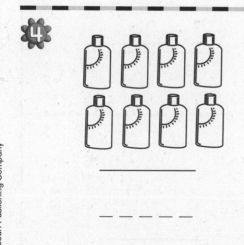

_____

- - - - - - - - -

_____

5

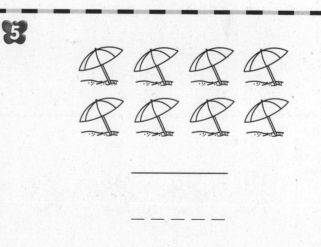

_____

- - - - - - - - -

_____

DIRECTIONS 1. Say the number. Trace the numbers.
2–5. Count and tell how many. Write the number.

Lesson Check (K.CC.3)

_____

- - - - - - - - -

_____

Spiral Review (K.CC.4b, K.CC.6)

_____   _____

- - - - - - - - -   - - - - - - - - -

_____   _____

_____

- - - - - - - - -

_____

DIRECTIONS 1. Count and tell how many bees. Write the number. **2.** Count and tell how many are in each set. Write the numbers. Compare the numbers. Circle the number that is greater. **3.** Count and tell how many beetles. Write the number.

P48 forty-eight

Name _____

Model and Count 9

COMMON CORE STANDARD—K.CC.5
Count to tell the number of objects.

9
nine

and

and

and

and

and

and

DIRECTIONS 1. Trace the number 9. Use two-color counters to model the different ways to make 9. Color to show the counters below. Write to show some pairs of numbers that make 9.

Chapter 3

forty-nine **P49**

Lesson Check (K.CC.5)

 1

9

nine

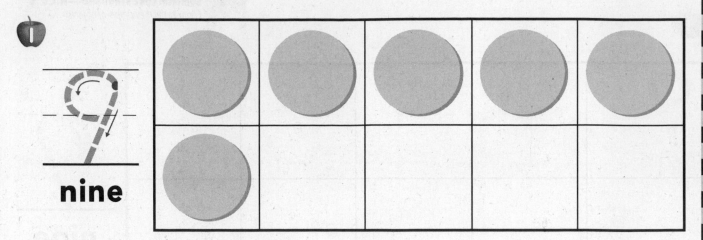

Spiral Review (K.CC.3, K.CC.6)

2

_____

- - - - - - - - - - -

_____

_____

- - - - - - - - - - -

_____

3

_____

- - - - - - - - - - -

_____

DIRECTIONS 1. Trace the number. How many more counters would you place in the ten frame to model a way to make 9? Draw the counters. **2.** Count and tell how many are in each set. Write the numbers. Compare the numbers. Circle the number that is greater. **3.** Count and tell how many. Write the number.

Count and Write to 9

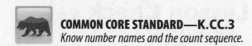

COMMON CORE STANDARD—K.CC.3
Know number names and the count sequence.

9 nine

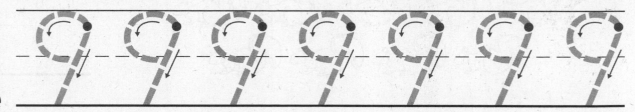

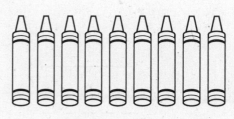

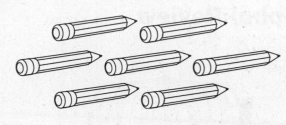

_____

- - - - - - -

_____

_____

- - - - - - -

_____

_____

- - - - - - -

_____

_____

- - - - - - -

_____

DIRECTIONS 1. Say the number. Trace the numbers.
2–5. Count and tell how many. Write the number.

Lesson Check (K.CC.3)

_____

- - - - - -

_____

Spiral Review (K.CC.3, K.CC.4b)

2

_____

- - - - - -

_____

3

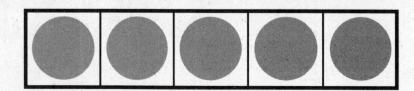

_____

- - - - - -

_____

DIRECTIONS 1. Count and tell how many squirrels. Write the number. **2.** How many birds are in the cage? Write the number. **3.** How many counters are there? Write the number.

Problem Solving • Numbers to 9

COMMON CORE STANDARD—K.CC.6
Compare numbers.

_____

- - - - - - -

_____

_____

- - - - - - -

_____

_____

- - - - - - -

_____

_____

- - - - - - -

_____

DIRECTIONS 1. Sally has six flowers. Three of the flowers are yellow. The rest are red. How many are yellow? Draw the flowers. Write the number beside each set of flowers. **2.** Tim has seven acorns. Don has a number of acorns that is two less than 7. How many acorns does Don have? Draw the acorns. Write the numbers.

Lesson Check (K.CC.6)

_____

- - - - - - - - -

_____

_____

- - - - - - - - -

_____

Spiral Review (K.CC.4b, K.CC.6)

_____

- - - - - - - - -

_____

_____   _____

- - - - - - - - -   - - - - - - - - -

_____   _____

DIRECTIONS **1.** Pete has 5 marbles. Jay has a number of marbles that is two more than 5. How many marbles does Jay have? Draw the marbles. Write the numbers. **2.** Count and tell how many books. **3.** Count and tell how many are in each set. Write the numbers. Compare the numbers. Circle the number that is greater.

Chapter 7

School-Home
Letter

Dear Family,

My class started Chapter 4 this week. In this chapter, I will learn how to show and compare numbers to 10.

Love, _____

Vocabulary

ten one more than nine

Home Activity

Place one button or penny in the ten frame below. Ask your child how many more are needed to make 10. Count aloud with your child as he or she places nine more buttons or pennies in the ten frame. Repeat the activity, starting with a different number each time.

Literature

Look for these books in the library. You and your child will enjoy these fun stories while learning more about the numbers 6 to 10.

Feast for 10 by Cathryn Falwell. Clarion Books, 1993.

Ten Black Dots by Donald Crews. Greenwillow Books, 1995.

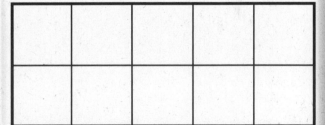

Carta
para la **casa**

Querida familia:

Mi clase comenzó el Capítulo 4 esta semana. En este capítulo, aprenderé mostrar y comparar números hasta el 10.

Con cariño, _____

Vocabulario

diez uno más que nueve

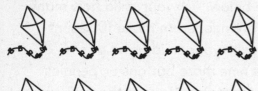

Actividad para la casa

Ponga un botón o una moneda de 1¢ en el cuadro de diez que está abajo. Pregúntele a su hijo cuántos más se necesitan para llegar a 10. Cuente en voz alta con su hijo mientras él coloca nueve botones o monedas de 1¢ más en el cuadro de diez. Repita la actividad y comience con un número diferente cada vez.

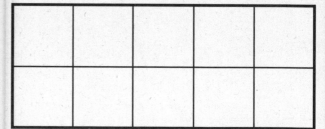

Literatura

Busquen estos libros en la biblioteca. Usted y su hijo se divertirán leyendo estos cuentos mientras aprenden más sobre los números del 6 al 10.

Feast for 10 by Cathryn Falwell. Clarion Books, 1993.

Ten Black Dots by Donald Crews. Greenwillow Books, 1995.

Model and Count 10

COMMON CORE STANDARD—K.CC.5
Count to tell the number of objects.

ten

and

and

and

and

DIRECTIONS Trace the number. Use counters to model the different ways to make 10. Color to show the counters below. Write to show some pairs of numbers that make 10.

Lesson Check (K.CC.5)

 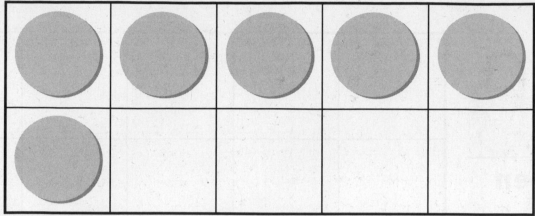

ten

Spiral Review (K.CC.6, K.CC.3)

_____

- - - - - - - - - -

_____

_____

- - - - - - - - - -

_____

....

_____

- - - - - - - - - -

_____

© Houghton Mifflin Harcourt Publishing Company

DIRECTIONS 1. Trace the number. How many more counters would you place in the ten frame to model a way to make 10? Draw the counters. 2. Count how many kites. Write the number. Draw to show a set of counters that has the same number as the set of kites. Write the number. 3. Count and tell how many. Write the number.

Name _____

Count and Write to 10

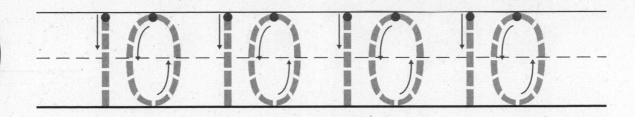

COMMON CORE STANDARD—K.CC.3
Know number names and the count sequence.

1

10
ten

 10 10 10 10

2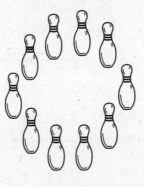

_____

- - - - - - - - -

_____

3

_____

- - - - - - - - -

_____

4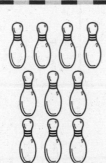

_____

- - - - - - - - -

_____

DIRECTIONS 1. Say the number. Trace the numbers.
2–4. Count and tell how many. Write the number.

Chapter 4

Lesson Check (K.CC.3)

_____

- - - - - - - - - - - -

_____

Spiral Review (K.CC.6, K.CC.4a)

_____   _____

- - - - - - - - -   - - - - - - - - -

_____   _____

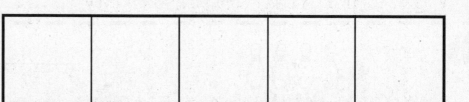

DIRECTIONS 1. Count and tell how many ears of corn. Write the number. 2. Count and tell how many are in each set. Write the numbers. Compare the numbers. Circle the number that is less. 3. How many counters would you place in the five frame? Trace the number.

P60 sixty

Name _____

Algebra • Ways to Make 10

COMMON CORE STANDARD—K.OA.4
Understand addition as putting together and adding to, and understand subtraction as taking apart and taking from.

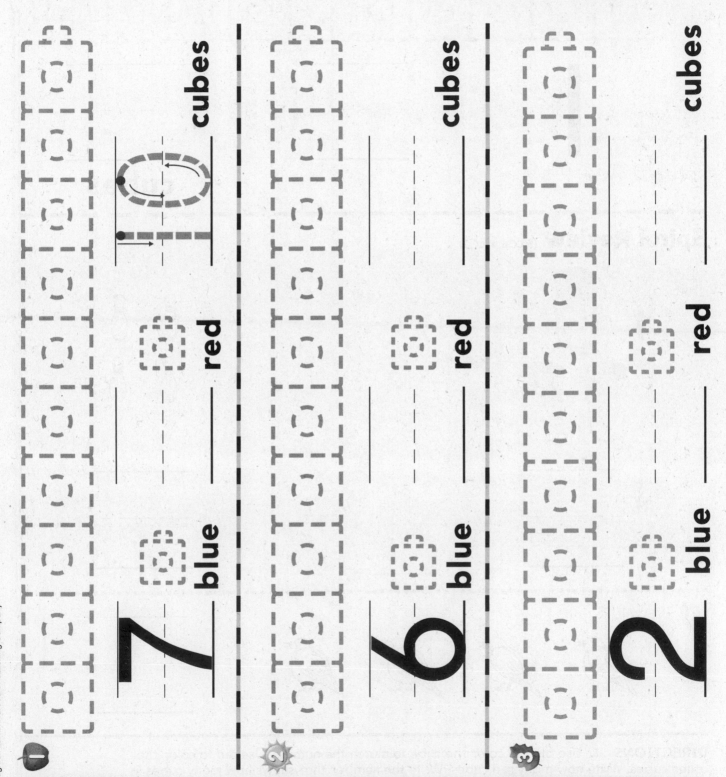

cubes — red — blue

1. 7

2. 6

3. 2

DIRECTIONS 1–3. Use blue to color the cubes to match the number. Use red to color the other cubes. Write how many red cubes. Trace or write the number that shows how many cubes in all.

Chapter 4

sixty-one **P61**

Lesson Check (K.OA.4)

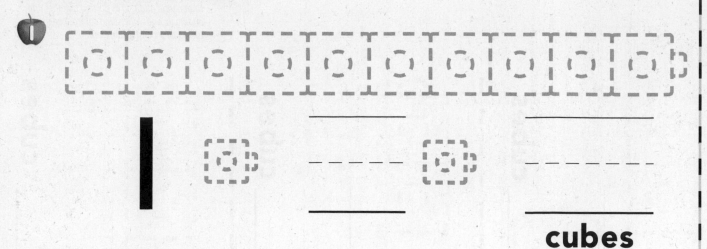

| cubes

Spiral Review (K.CC.6, K.CC.3)

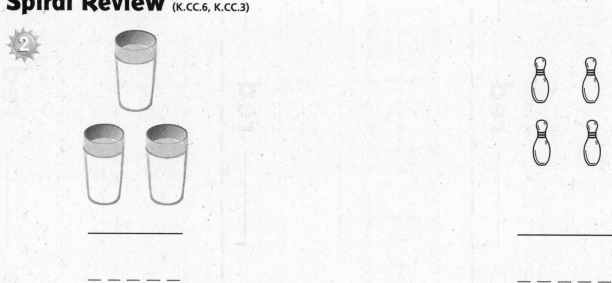

DIRECTIONS **I.** Use blue to color the cube to match the number. Use red to color the other cubes. Write how many red cubes. Write the number that shows how many cubes in all. **2.** Count and tell how many are in each set. Write the numbers. Compare the numbers. Circle the number that is greater. **3.** How many birds are there? Write the number.

Name _____

Count and Order to 10

 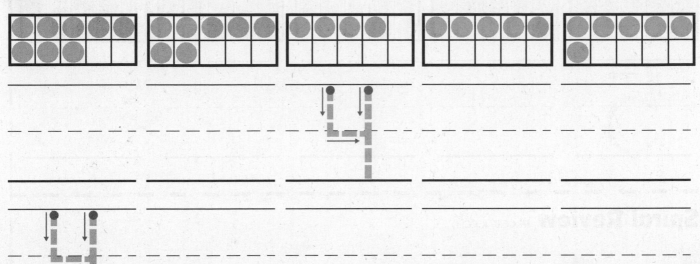

COMMON CORE STANDARD—K.CC.2
Know number names and the count sequence.

 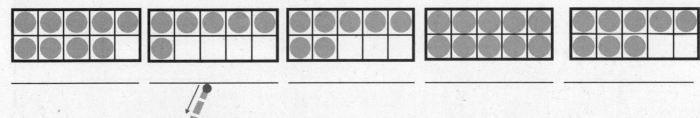

DIRECTIONS 1–2. Count the dots in the ten frames. Trace
or write the numbers. Write the numbers in order as you count
forward from the dashed number.

Lesson Check (K.CC.2)

5

Spiral Review (K.CC.6, K.CC.3)

DIRECTIONS **1.** Count the dots in the ten frames. Trace the number. Write the numbers in order as you count forward from the dashed number. **2.** Count and tell how many are in each set. Write the numbers. Compare the numbers. Circle the number that is less. **3.** How many counters are there? Write the number.

Problem Solving • Compare by Matching Sets to 10

 COMMON CORE STANDARD—K.CC.6
Compare numbers.

①

_____

- - - - - - - - -

_____

_____

- - - - - - - - -

_____

②

_____

- - - - - - - - -

_____

_____

- - - - - - - - -

_____

DIRECTIONS   1. Kim has 7 red balloons. Jake has 3 blue balloons. Who has fewer balloons? Use cube trains to model the sets of balloons. Compare the cube trains. Write how many. Circle the number that is less.   **2.** Meg has 8 red beads. Beni has 5 blue beads. Who has more beads? Use cube trains to model the sets of beads. Compare the cube trains by matching. Draw and color the cube trains. Write how many. Circle the number that is greater.

Chapter 4

Lesson Check (K.CC.6)

_____

_____

_____

- - - - - - - - -

_____

Spiral Review (K.CC.6, K.CC.4b)

2

_____   _____

- - - - - - - - -   - - - - - - - - -

_____   _____

3

_____

- - - - - - - - -

_____

DIRECTIONS 1. Mia has 6 red marbles. Zack has 2 blue marbles. Who has more marbles? Use cube trains to model the sets of marbles. Compare the cube trains by matching. Draw and color the cube trains. Write how many. Circle the number that is greater. 2. Count and tell how many are in each set. Write the numbers. Compare the numbers. Circle the number that is greater. 3. Count and tell how many. Write the number.

P66 sixty-six

Compare by Counting Sets to 10

COMMON CORE STANDARD—K.CC.6
Compare numbers.

 1

_____

- - - - - - - - - -

_____

_____

- - - - - - - - - -

_____

2

_____

- - - - - - - - - -

_____

_____

- - - - - - - - - -

_____

3

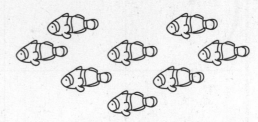

_____

- - - - - - - - - -

_____

_____

- - - - - - - - - -

_____

DIRECTIONS Count how many in each set. Write the number of objects in each set. Compare the numbers. **1–2.** Circle the number that is less. **3.** Circle the number that is greater.

Lesson Check (K.CC.6)

1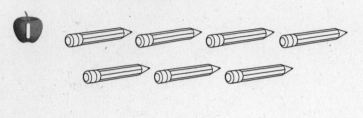

_____

— — — — — —

_____

Spiral Review (K.CC.3, K.CC.5)

2

_____

— — — — — —

_____

3

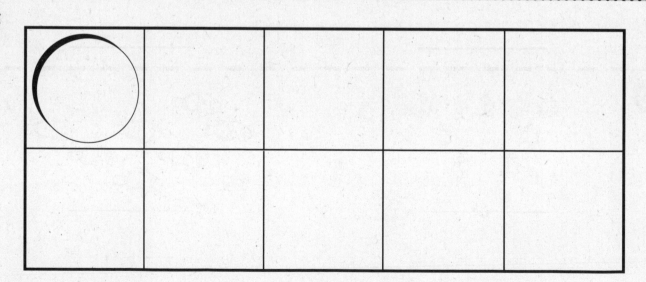

DIRECTIONS **1.** Count and tell how many are in each set. Write the numbers. Compare the numbers. Circle the number that is less. **2.** How many whistles are there? Write the number. **3.** How many more counters would you place in the ten frame to show a way to make 6? Draw the counters.

Name _____

Compare Two Numbers

COMMON CORE STANDARD—K.CC.7
Compare numbers.

1   8   5

2   10   7

3   6   9

4   4   6

5   8   7

6   5   3

DIRECTIONS 1–3. Look at the numbers. Think about the counting order as you compare the numbers. Circle the greater number. **4–6.** Look at the numbers. Think about the counting order as you compare the numbers. Circle the number that is less.

7   8

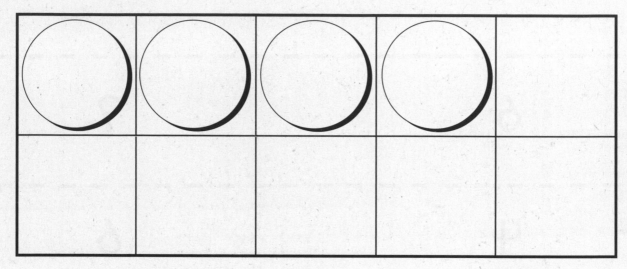

_____

- - - - - - - - - - - -

_____

DIRECTIONS 1. Look at the numbers. Think about the counting order as you compare the numbers. Circle the greater number. 2. How many more counters would you place in the ten frame to show a way to make 8? Draw the counters. 3. How many birds are there? Write the number.

School-Home
Letter

Dear Family,

My class started Chapter 5 this week. In this chapter, I will learn how to show addition.

Love, _____

Vocabulary

add to put together one set with another set

o	o	o	o	o

plus (+) a symbol that shows addition

plus
↓
$3 + 2 = 5$

Home Activity

Invite your child to act out addition word problems. For example, your child can show you four socks, add two more socks, and then tell you the addition sentence.

$4 + 2 = 6$

Literature

Look for these books at the library. You and your child will enjoy counting and adding objects in these interactive books.

Rooster's Off to See the World by Eric Carle. Simon & Schuster, 1991.

Anno's Counting Book by Mitsumasa Anno. HarperCollins, 1986.

Carta
para la casa

Querida familia:

Mi clase comenzó el Capítulo 5 esta semana. En este capítulo aprenderé todo sobre la suma.

Con cariño, _____

Vocabulario

sumar agregar un conjunto a otro

$3 + 2 = 5$

más (+) signo que indica suma

más
↓
$3 + 2 = 5$

Actividad para la casa

Anime a su hijo a representar problemas de suma. Por ejemplo, puede mostrar cuatro calcetines, agregar dos calcetines más y luego decir el enunciado de la suma.

$4 + 2 = 6$

Busquen otros objetos que puedan usarse para representar cuentos de resta.

Literatura

Busquen estos libros en la biblioteca. Usted y su hijo disfrutarán estos libros interactivos que sirven para reforzar las destrezas de suma.

Rooster's Off to See the World
por Eric Carle. Simon & Schuster, 1991.

Anno's Counting Book
by Mitsumasa Anno. HarperCollins, 1986.

Name _____

Addition: Add To

COMMON CORE STANDARD—K.OA.1
Understand addition as putting together and adding to, and understand subtraction as taking apart and taking from.

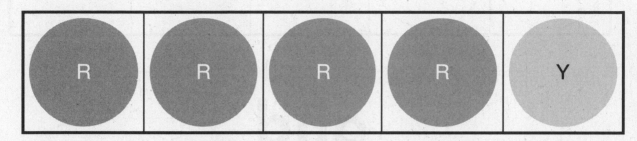

_____ and _____

- - - - -   - - - - -

_____   _____

_____

- - - - -

_____

DIRECTIONS 1. There are four red counters in the five frame. One yellow counter is added. R is for red, and Y is for yellow. How many are there of each color counter? Write the numbers. **2.** Write the number that shows how many counters are in the five frame now.

Chapter 5

Lesson Check (K.OA.1)

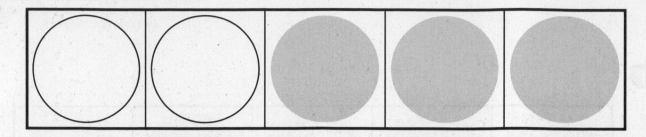

_____   _____

- - - - - -   **and**   - - - - - -

_____   _____

Spiral Review (K.CC.3, K.CC.6)

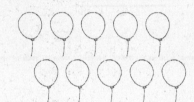

_____

- - - - - - - - -

_____

_____   _____

- - - - - -   - - - - - -

_____   _____

DIRECTIONS 1. How many of each color counter? Write the numbers.
2. Count and tell how many balloons. Write the number.   3. Count and
tell how many in each set. Write the numbers. Compare the numbers.
Circle the number that is less.

Addition: Put Together

COMMON CORE STANDARD—K.OA.1
Understand addition as putting together and adding to, and understand subtraction as taking apart and taking from.

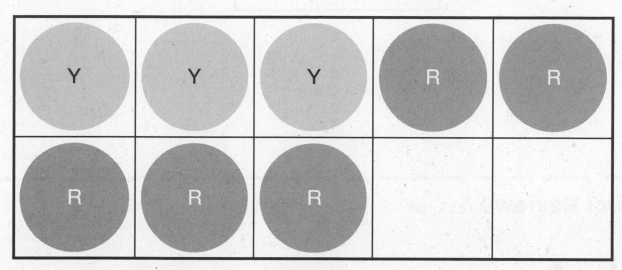

3   **and**   **5**

_____   _____

┊   ┊   _____

_____   ┊   _____

          _____

          _____

DIRECTIONS Roy has three yellow counters and five red counters. How many counters does he have in all? **I.** Place counters in the ten frame to model the sets that are put together. Y is for yellow, and R is for red. Write the numbers and trace the symbol. Write the number to show how many in all.

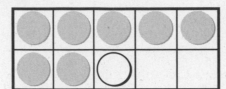

6 _ _ _ _ 8 _ _ _ _ 10

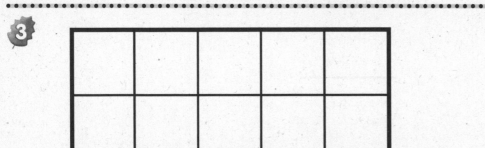

DIRECTIONS **1.** What numbers show the sets that are put together? Write the numbers and trace the symbol. **2.** Count the dots in the ten frames. Begin with 6. Write the numbers in order as you count forward. **3.** Paul has a number of counters two less than seven. Draw the counters in the ten frame. Write the number.

Name _____

Problem Solving • Act Out
Addition Problems

COMMON CORE STANDARD—K.OA.1
Understand addition as putting together and adding to, and understand subtraction as taking apart and taking from.

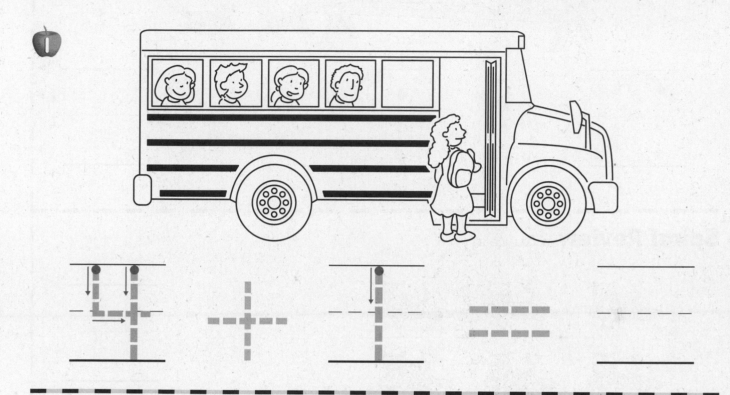

1

$$4 + 1 = \_\_\_$$

2

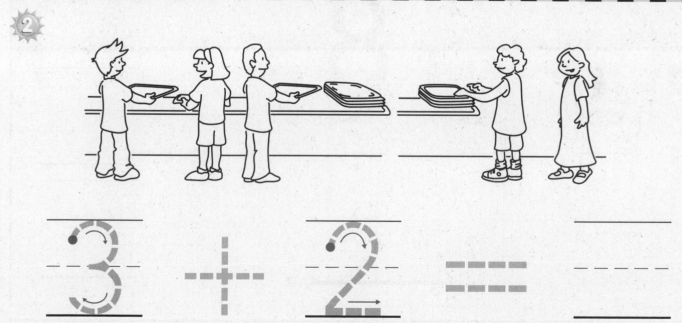

$$3 + 2 = \_\_\_$$

DIRECTIONS 1–2. Tell an addition word problem about the children. Trace the numbers and the symbols. Write the number that shows how many children in all.

© Houghton Mifflin Harcourt Publishing Company

Lesson Check (K.OA.1)

$$3 + 2 = \text{\_\_\_}$$

Spiral Review (K.CC.3, K.CC.6)

DIRECTIONS **1.** Tell an addition word problem. Trace the numbers and the symbols. Write the number that shows how many cats in all. **2.** Count and tell how many tigers. Write the number. **3.** Count how many bears. Write the number. Draw to show a set of counters that has the same number as the set of bears. Write the number.

Algebra • Model and Draw
Addition Problems

COMMON CORE STANDARD—K.OA.5
Understand addition as putting together and adding to, and understand subtraction as taking apart and taking from.

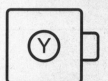

  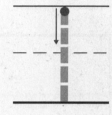

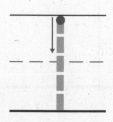  

DIRECTIONS 1–2. Place cubes as shown. B is for blue, and Y is for yellow. Tell an addition word problem. Model to show the cubes put together. Draw the cube train. Trace and write the sum to complete the addition sentence.

Chapter 5

Lesson Check (K.OA.5)

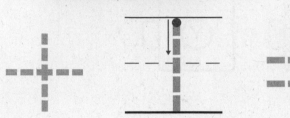

Spiral Review (K.CC.3, K.CC.5)

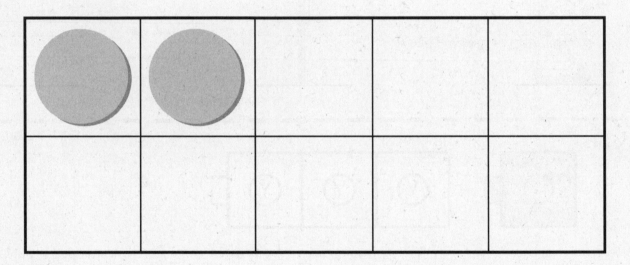

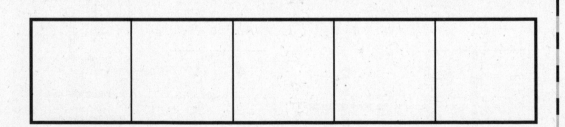

DIRECTIONS **1.** Look at the cube train. Tell an addition word problem. Trace and write to complete the addition sentence. **2.** How many more counters would you place to model a way to make 7? Draw the counters. **3.** Draw counters to make a set that shows the number.

Algebra • Write Addition Sentences for 10

COMMON CORE STANDARD—K.OA.5
Understand addition as putting together and adding to, and understand subtraction as taking apart and taking from.

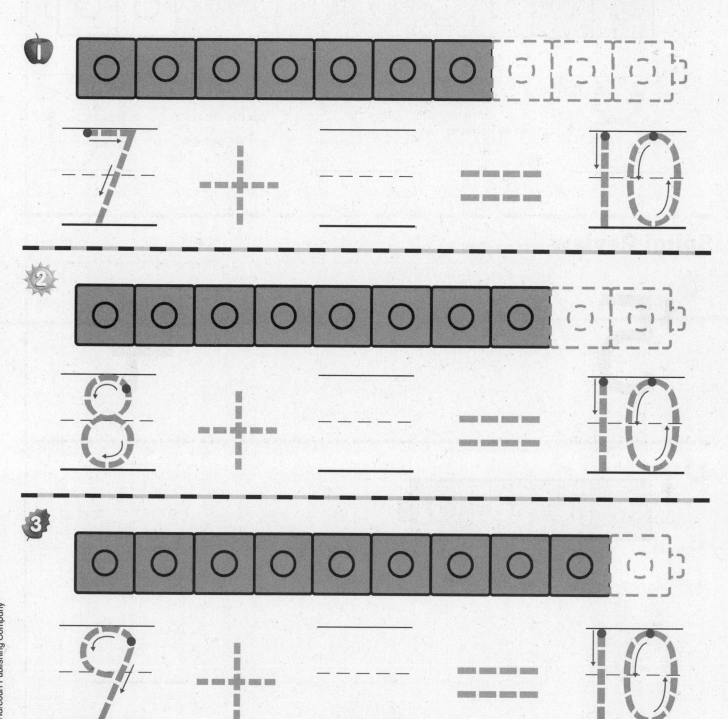

DIRECTIONS 1–3. Look at the cube train. How many gray cubes do you see? How many blue cubes do you need to add to make 10? Use blue to color those cubes. Write and trace to show this as an addition sentence.

Chapter 5

Lesson Check (K.OA.4)

1

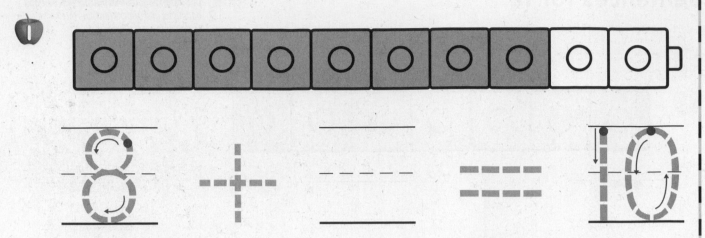

Spiral Review (K.CC.6, K.CC.7)

2

5   4

3

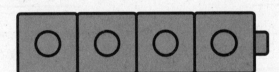

DIRECTIONS **1.** Look at the cube train. How many white cubes are added to the gray cubes to make 10? Write and trace to show this as an addition sentence.   **2.** Which number is less? Circle the number.   **3.** How many cubes are there? Write the number. Model a cube train that has the same number of cubes. Draw the cube train. Write how many.

Algebra • Write Addition Sentences

COMMON CORE STANDARD—K.OA.5
Understand addition as putting together and adding to, and understand subtraction as taking apart and taking from.

1

3 + ___ = 5

2

1 + ___ = 4

3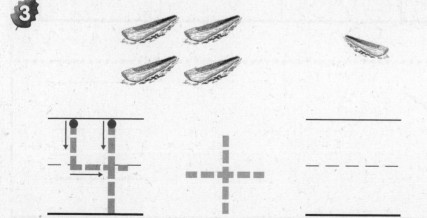

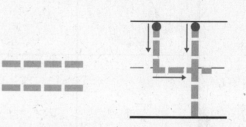

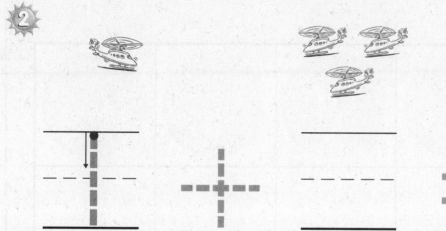

4 + ___ = 5

DIRECTIONS I–3. Tell an addition word problem about the sets. Circle the set you start with. How many are being added to the set? How many are there now? Write and trace to complete the addition sentence.

Spiral Review (K.CC.3, K.CC.5)

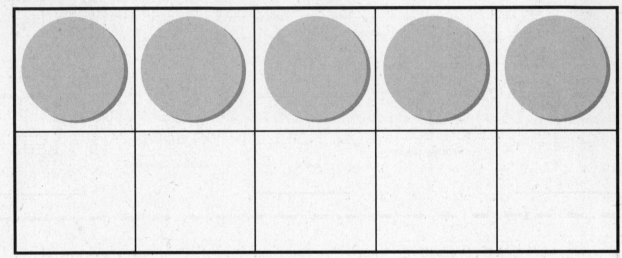

DIRECTIONS 1. Tell an addition word problem about the sets. Write and trace to complete the addition sentence. **2.** How many more counters would you place to model a way to make 8? Draw the counters. **3.** How many paintbrushes are there? Write the number.

Algebra • Write More Addition Sentences

COMMON CORE STANDARD—K.OA.2
Understand addition as putting together and adding to, and understand subtraction as taking apart and taking from.

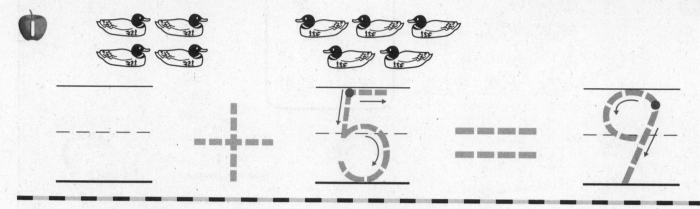

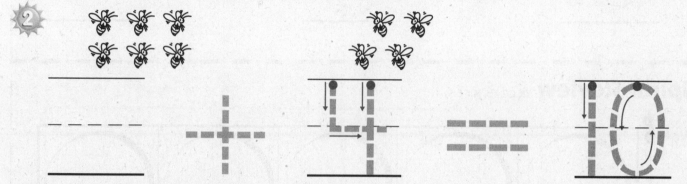

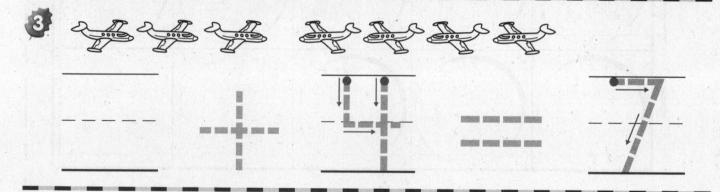

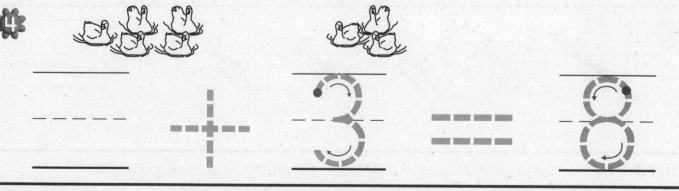

DIRECTIONS 1–4. Tell an addition word problem. Circle the set being added. How many are in the set to start with? Write and trace to complete the addition sentence.

Lesson Check

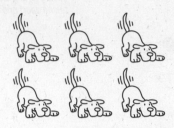 

_ _ _ _ _  $+$ 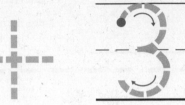 **3** $=$  **9**

_ _ _ _ _

Spiral Review (K.CC.4b, K.CC.5)

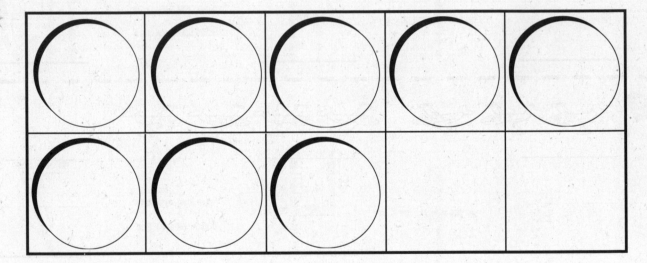

_ _ _ _ _

DIRECTIONS 1. Tell an addition word problem about the sets. Write and trace to complete the addition sentence. 2. How many more counters would you place to model a way to make 9? Draw the counters. 3. Count and tell how many trumpets. Write the number.

Algebra • Number Pairs to 5

COMMON CORE STANDARD—K.OA.3
Understand addition as putting together and adding to, and understand subtraction as taking apart and taking from.

1

3 = ___ + ___

2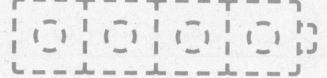

4 = ___ + ___

3

5 = ___ + ___

DIRECTIONS 1–3. Look at the number at the beginning of the addition sentence. Place two colors of cubes on the cube train to show a number pair for that number. Complete the addition sentence to show a number pair. Color the cube train to match the addition sentence.

Lesson Check (K.OA.3)

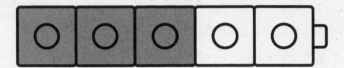

$$5 \ === \ \text{-----} \ + \ \text{-----}$$

Spiral Review (K.CC.5, K.CC.6)

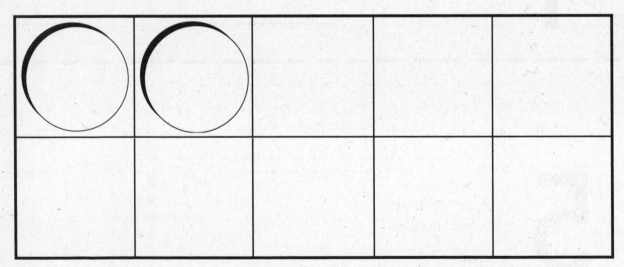

DIRECTIONS 1. Complete the addition sentence to show the numbers that match the cube train. 2. Count the number of turtles in each set. Circle the set that has the greater number of turtles. 3. How many more counters would you place to model a way to make 6? Draw the counters.

Algebra • Number Pairs for 6 and 7

COMMON CORE STANDARD—K.OA.3
Understand addition as putting together and adding to, and understand subtraction as taking apart and taking from.

$$6 = \underline{\qquad} + \underline{\qquad}$$

$$7 = \underline{\qquad} + \underline{\qquad}$$

DIRECTIONS 1–2. Look at the number at the beginning of the addition sentence. Place two colors of cubes on the cube train to show a number pair for that number. Complete the addition sentence to show a number pair. Color the cube train to match the addition sentence.

Chapter 5

Lesson Check (K.OA.3)

7 = _____ _____ + _____

Spiral Review (K.CC.5, K.CC.3)

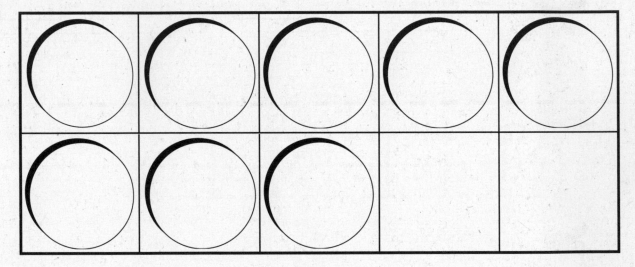

_____
_____
_____

DIRECTIONS 1. Complete the addition sentence to show the numbers that match the cube train. **2.** How many more counters would you place to model a way to make 10? Draw the counters. **3.** Count and tell how many hats. Write the number.

P90 ninety

Algebra • Number Pairs for 8

COMMON CORE STANDARD—K.OA.3
Understand addition as putting together and adding to, and understand subtraction as taking apart and taking from.

8 ▬▬▬   _____ + _____

8 ▬▬▬   _____ + _____

8 ▬▬▬   _____ + _____

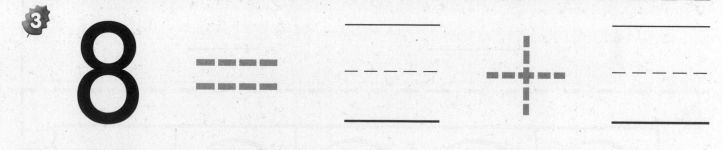

8 ▬▬▬   _____ + _____

DIRECTIONS Use two colors of cubes to make a cube train to show the number pairs that make 8. 1–4. Complete the addition sentence to show a number pair for 8. Color the cube train to match the addition sentence in Exercise 4.

Chapter 5

ninety-one **P91**

© Houghton Mifflin Harcourt Publishing Company

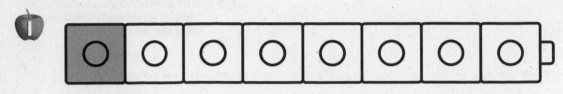

8 = ___ + ___

___

___

___

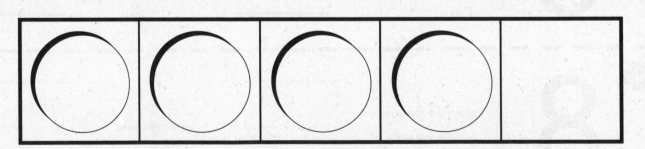

DIRECTIONS 1. Complete the addition sentence to show the numbers that match the cube train. 2. Count and tell how many in each set. Write the numbers. Compare the numbers. Circle the number that is greater. 3. How many more counters would you place in the five frame to show a way to make 5? Draw the counters.

Algebra • Number Pairs for 9

COMMON CORE STANDARD—K.OA.3
Understand addition as putting together and adding to, and understand subtraction as taking apart and taking from.

DIRECTIONS Use two colors of cubes to make a cube train to show the number pairs that make 9. 1–4. Complete the addition sentence to show a number pair for 9. Color the cube train to match the addition sentence in Exercise 4.

Chapter 5

Lesson Check (K.OA.3)

$9 =$ _____ $+$ _____

. . . .

Spiral Review (K.CC.3, K.CC.6)

_____

- - - - - - -

_____

_____   _____

- - - - - - -   - - - - - - -

_____

DIRECTIONS 1. Complete the addition sentence to show the numbers that match the cube train. **2.** Count how many birds. Write the number. **3.** Count and tell how many in each set. Write the numbers. Compare the numbers. Circle the number that is less.

Algebra • Number Pairs for 10

COMMON CORE STANDARD—K.OA.3
Understand addition as putting together and adding to, and understand subtraction as taking apart and taking from.

1. 10 = _____ + _____

2. 10 = _____ + _____

3. 10 = _____ + _____

4. 10 = _____ + _____

DIRECTIONS Use two colors of cubes to build a cube train to show the number pairs that make 10. **1–4.** Complete the addition sentence to show a number pair for 10. Color the cube train to match the addition sentence in Exercise 4.

Chapter 5

Lesson Check (K.OA.3)

1

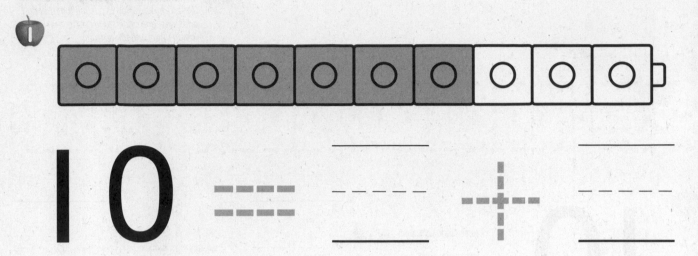

$$10 = \underline{\hspace{2cm}} + \underline{\hspace{2cm}}$$

Spiral Review (K.CC.4c, K.OA.4)

2

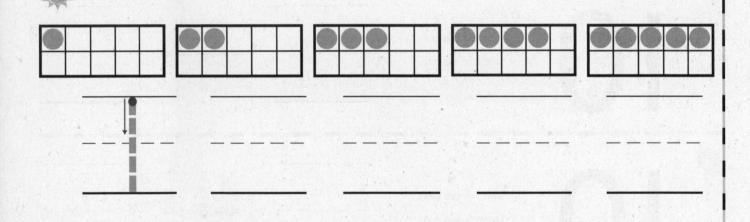

3

DIRECTIONS 1. Complete the addition sentence to show the numbers that match the cube train. 2. Count the dots in the ten frames. Trace the number. Write the numbers in order as you count forward from the dashed number. 3. Use blue and red to color the cubes to show a way to make 10.

School-Home Letter

Dear Family,

My class started Chapter 6 this week. In this chapter, I will learn how to show subtraction.

Love, _____

Vocabulary

minus (−) a symbol that shows subtraction

minus
$$3 \overset{\downarrow}{-} 2 = 1$$

subtract to take apart or take from

Home Activity

Invite your child to act out subtraction word problems. For example, your child can show you five spoons, take away two spoons, and then tell you the subtraction sentence.

$$5 - 2 = 3$$

Literature

Look for these books at the library. You and your child will enjoy these books that strengthen subtraction skills.

Elevator Magic by Stuart J. Murphy. HarperCollins, 1997.

Ten Red Apples by Pat Hutchins. Greenwillow Books, 2000.

Carta
para la casa

Querida familia:

Mi clase comenzó el Capítulo 6 esta semana. En este capítulo aprenderé cómo mostrar una resta.

Con cariño, _____

Vocabulario

menos (−) signo que indica una resta

signo de resta

$$3 - 2 = 1$$

restar quitar

Actividad para la casa

Anime a su hijo para que represente problemas de resta. Por ejemplo, su hijo puede mostrarle 5 cucharas, quitar 2 cucharas y luego decirle el enunciado de la resta.

$$5 - 2 = 3$$

Literatura

Busque este libro en una biblioteca. Su hijo y usted disfrutarán de este libro interactivo que fortalecerá las destrezas para restar.

Elevator Magic por Stuart J. Murphy. HarperTrophy, 1997.

Ten Red Apples por Pat Hutchins. Greenwillow Books, 2000.

Subtraction: Take From

COMMON CORE STANDARD—K.OA.1
Understand addition as putting together and adding to, and understand subtraction as taking apart and taking from.

_____   _____

- - - - - -   - - - - - -

_____   **take away**   _____

_____

- - - - - -

_____

DIRECTIONS 1. Tell a subtraction word problem about the children. Write the number that shows how many children in all. Write the number that shows how many children are leaving. Write the number that shows how many children are left.

Chapter 6

Lesson Check (K.OA.1)

3 take away 1

_____

- - - - - - - - - -

_____

Spiral Review (K.CC.5, K.OA.2)

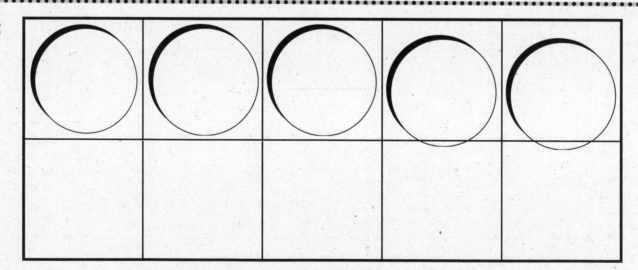

DIRECTIONS 1. Tell a subtraction word problem about the frogs. Write the number that shows how many frogs are left. 2. Tell an addition word problem about the birds. Write and trace to complete the addition sentence. 3. How many more counters would you place to model a way to make 8? Draw the counters.

Subtraction: Take Apart

COMMON CORE STANDARD—K.OA.1
Understand addition as putting together and adding to, and understand subtraction as taking apart and taking from.

9   minus   3

_____   _____

_ _ _ _ _   **___**   _ _ _ _ _

_____   _____

_____

_ _ _ _ _

_____

DIRECTIONS 1. Listen to the subtraction word problem. Jane has nine counters. Three of her counters are red. The rest of her counters are yellow. How many are yellow? Place nine counters in the ten frame. Draw and color the counters. Write the number that shows how many in all. Write the number that shows how many are red. Write the number that shows how many are yellow.

Chapter 6

one hundred one **P101**

Lesson Check <small>(K.OA.1)</small>

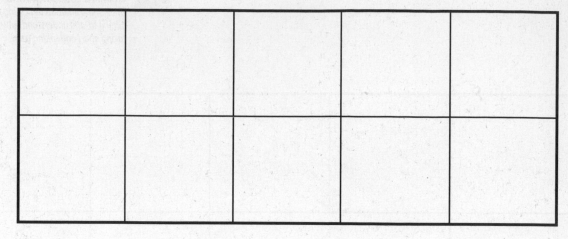

$$8 - 2$$

_____

- - - - - - - -

_____

Spiral Review <small>(K.CC.6)</small>

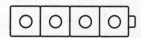

- - - - - - - -

_____

- - - - - - - -

_____

_____

- - - - - - - -

_____

DIRECTIONS 1. Clyde has eight counters. Two of his counters are yellow. The rest of his counters are red. How many are red? Draw and color the counters. Write the number that shows how many are red. **2.** Write the number that is one greater than the number of leaves. **3.** Compare the cube trains. Write how many. Circle the number that is greater.

Problem Solving • Act Out Subtraction Problems

COMMON CORE STANDARD—K.OA.1
Understand addition as putting together and adding to, and understand subtraction as taking apart and taking from.

$$3 - 1 = \underline{\hspace{1cm}}$$

$$4 - 3 = \underline{\hspace{1cm}}$$

DIRECTIONS **1.** Tell a subtraction word problem about the beavers. Trace the numbers and the symbols. Write the number that shows how many beavers are left. **2.** Draw to tell a story about the subtraction sentence. Write how many are left. Tell a friend about your drawing.

Chapter 6

Lesson Check (K.OA.1)

 5 — 4 = ___

Spiral Review (K.CC.3, K.CC.5)

___

- - -

___

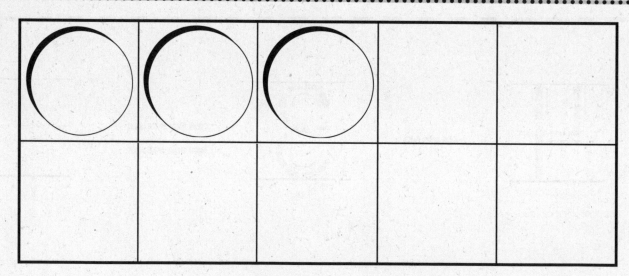

DIRECTIONS 1. Tell a subtraction word problem about the birds. Trace the numbers and the symbols. Write the number that shows how many birds are left. **2.** Count and tell how many bees. Write the number. **3.** How many more counters would you place to model a way to make 7? Draw the counters.

Algebra • Model and Draw
Subtraction Problems

COMMON CORE STANDARD—K.OA.5
Understand addition as putting together and adding to, and understand subtraction as taking apart and taking from.

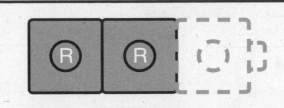

   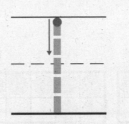   

   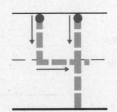   

DIRECTIONS   1. Model a three-cube train. Two cubes are red and the rest are blue. Take apart the cube train to show how many cubes are blue. Draw and color the cube trains. Trace and write to complete the subtraction sentence. **2.** Model a five-cube train. One cube is yellow and the rest are green. Take apart the train to show how many cubes are green. Draw and color the cube trains. Trace and write to complete the subtraction sentence.

Chapter 6

Lesson Check (K.OA.5)

 —

$5 - 3 =$ _____

Spiral Review (K.CC.2, K.OA.3)

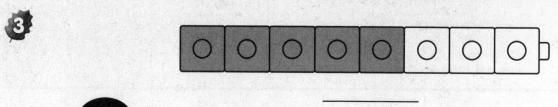

5 _____ 7 _____ 9

8 $=$ _____ _____ $+$ _____

DIRECTIONS 1. Ellie makes the cube train shown. She takes the cube train apart to show how many cubes are gray. Trace and write to show the subtraction sentence for Ellie's cube train. 2. Count the dots in the ten frames. Begin with 5. Write the numbers in order as you count forward. 3. Complete the addition sentence to show the numbers that match the cube train.

Algebra • Write Subtraction Sentences

 COMMON CORE STANDARD—K.OA.5
Understand addition as putting together and adding to, and understand subtraction as taking apart and taking from.

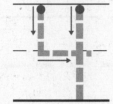 — ___ = ___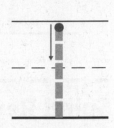

 ___   ___

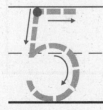  ___  ___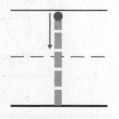

DIRECTIONS 1–3. Listen to the subtraction word problem about the animals. There are _____ _____. _____ are taken from the set. Now there are _____. How many are taken from the set? Circle and mark an X to show how many are being taken from the set. Trace and write to complete the subtraction sentence.

Lesson Check (K.OA.5)

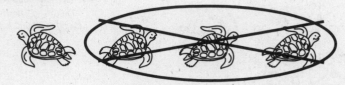

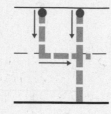

Spiral Review (K.CC.5, K.CC.6)

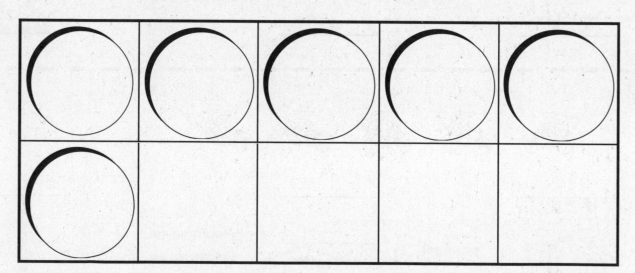

DIRECTIONS **1.** Trace and write to show the subtraction sentence for the set. **2.** Count the number of counters in each set. Circle the set that has the greater number of counters. **3.** How many more counters would you place to model a way to make 9? Draw the counters.

Algebra • Write More Subtraction Sentences

COMMON CORE STANDARD—K.OA.2
Understand addition as putting together and adding to, and understand subtraction as taking apart and taking from.

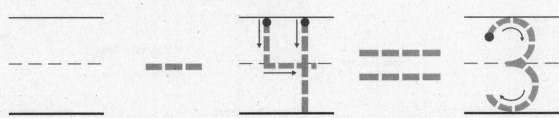

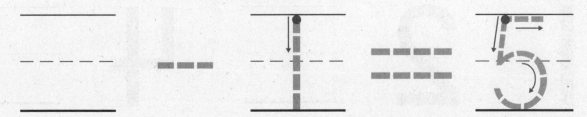

DIRECTIONS   I–3. Listen to a subtraction word problem about the birds. There are some birds. _____ birds are taken from the set. Now there are _____ birds. How many birds in all did you start with? Write the number to complete the subtraction sentence.

Lesson Check (K.OA.2)

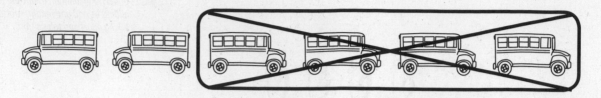

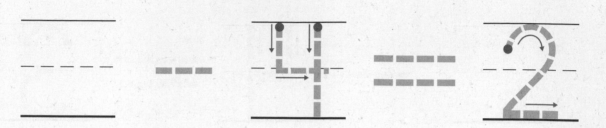

Spiral Review (K.CC.3, K.CC.4c)

_____

- - - - - - -

_____

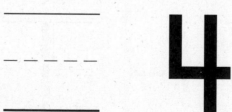

1   2   _ _ _   4   _ _ _

DIRECTIONS **1.** Trace and write to show the subtraction sentence for the buses. **2.** How many lunch boxes are there? Write the number. **3.** Count the dots in the ten frames. Begin with 1. Write the numbers in order as you count forward.

Name _____

Algebra • Addition and Subtraction

COMMON CORE STANDARD—K.OA.2
Understand addition as putting together and adding to, and understand subtraction as taking apart and taking from.

_____ + _____ = _____

- -

_____ _____ = _____

DIRECTIONS 1–2. Tell an addition or subtraction word problem. Use cubes to add or subtract. Complete the number sentence.

Chapter 6

one hundred eleven **P111**

Lesson Check (K.OA.2)

_____   _____   _____

- - -   - - -   = = =
                    = = =

_____   _____   _____

Spiral Review (K.CC.7, K.OA.3)

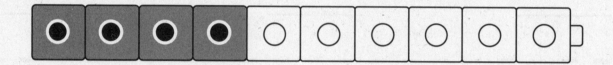

10

_____   _____   _____

= = =   - - -   + +   - - -
= = =

8   9

DIRECTIONS 1. Tell a subtraction word problem. Use cubes to subtract. Complete the number sentence. 2. Complete the addition sentence to show the numbers that match the cube train. 3. Compare the numbers. Circle the number that is greater.

School-Home Letter

Dear Family,

My class started Chapter 7 this week. In this chapter, I will learn how to show, count, and write numbers 11 to 19.

Love, _____

Vocabulary

eleven 10 ones and 1 one

sixteen 10 ones and 6 ones

nineteen 10 ones and 9 ones

Home Activity

Draw a ten frame on a sheet of paper. Write numbers 11 to 19 on small pieces of paper and place them face down in a pile. Have your child turn over the cards and use small objects, such as pennies, to model the numbers.

12

Literature

Look for this book at the library. You and your child will have fun looking at the pages while building your child's counting skills.

Bears at the Beach: Counting 10 to 20 by Niki Yektai. Millbrook Press, 2001.

Carta para la casa

Querida familia:

Mi clase comenzó el Capítulo 7 esta semana. En este capítulo, aprenderé cómo mostrar, contar y escribir los números del 11 al 19.

Con cariño, _____

Vocabulario

once uno más que diez

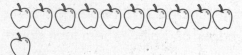

dieciséis uno más que quince

diecinueve uno más que dieciocho

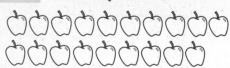

Actividad para la casa

Dibuje dos cuadros de diez, uno al lado del otro, en una hoja de papel. Escriba los números del 11 al 19 en pequeños trozos de papel y póngalos boca abajo en una pila. Pídale a su hijo que dé vuelta las cartas y que use objetos pequeños como monedas de 1¢ para representar los números.

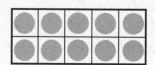

12

Literatura

Busque estos libros en la biblioteca. Usted y su hijo se divertirán mirando las páginas mientras refuerzan las destrezas de contar.

Bears at the Beach: Counting 10 to 20
por Niki Yektai.
Millbrook Press, 2001.

Model and Count 11 and 12

COMMON CORE STANDARD—K.NBT.1
Work with numbers 11–19 to gain foundations for place value.

  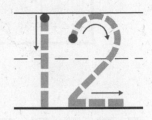

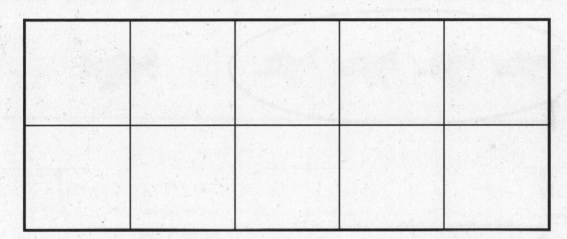

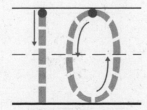 **ones and** _____ **ones**

DIRECTIONS 1. Count and tell how many. Trace the number. **2.** Use counters to show the number 12. Draw the counters. **3.** Look at the counters you drew. How many ones are in the ten frame? Trace the number. How many more ones are there? Write the number.

Lesson Check (K.NBT.1)

 1

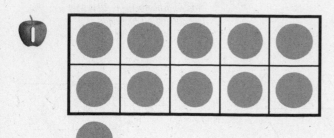

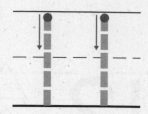

Spiral Review (K.CC.6, K.OA.5)

2

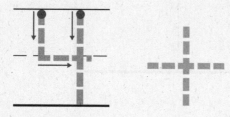  

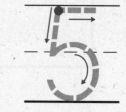

3

○ ○ ○ _____

_ _ _ _

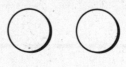

_____

DIRECTIONS 1. Count and tell how many. Trace the number. 2. Write and trace to show the addition sentence for the sets of airplanes. 3. Count and tell how many in each set. Write the numbers. Compare the numbers. Circle the number that is less..

Name _____

Count and Write 11 and 12

COMMON CORE STANDARD—K.CC.3
Know number names and the count sequence.

 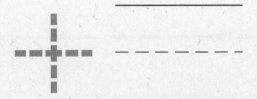

_____

_ _ _ _ _ _ _ _ _ _

_____

_____   _____   _____

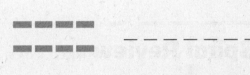

_____   _____   _____

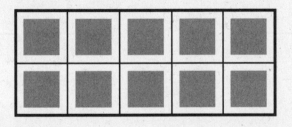

_____

_ _ _ _ _ _ _ _ _ _

_____

_____   _____   _____

_____   _____   _____

DIRECTIONS **1.** Count and tell how many. Write the number.
2. Look at the ten ones and some more ones in Exercise 1.
Complete the addition sentence to match. **3.** Count and tell how
many. Write the number. **4.** Look at the ten ones and some more
ones in Exercise 3. Complete the addition sentence to match.

Lesson Check (K.CC.3)

 1

Spiral Review (K.CC.3, K.OA.5)

 2

  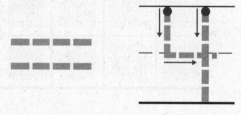

 3

DIRECTIONS **1.** Look at the ten ones and some more ones. Complete the addition sentence to match. **2.** Trace and write to show the subtraction sentence for the fish. **3.** How many birds are there? Write the number.

Model and Count 13 and 14

COMMON CORE STANDARD—K.NBT.1
*Work with numbers 11–19 to gain
foundations for place value.*

 1

14
fourteen

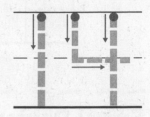

 2

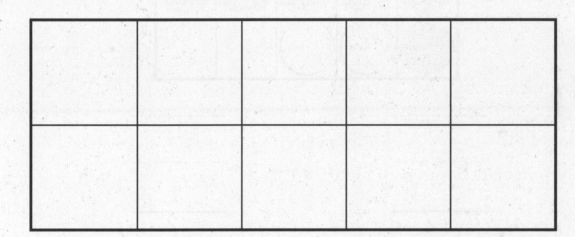

3

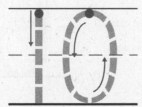 **ones and** _____ **ones**

DIRECTIONS 1. Count and tell how many. Trace the number. 2. Use counters to show
the number 14. Draw the counters. 3. Look at the counters you drew. How many ones are
in the ten frame? Trace the number. How many more ones are there? Write the number.

Lesson Check (K.NBT.1)

 1

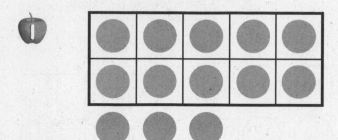

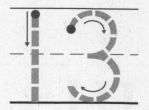

Spiral Review (K.OA.1, K.OA.2)

2

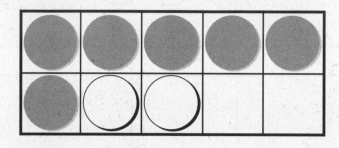

3

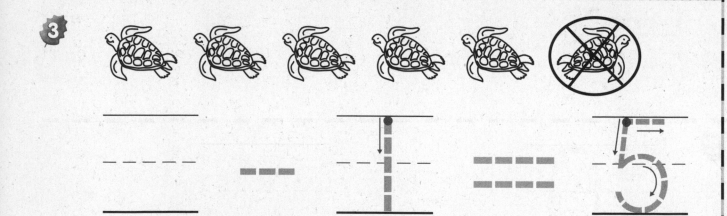

DIRECTIONS 1. Count and tell how many. Trace the number. 2. Show the sets that are put together. Trace the numbers and trace the symbol. 3. Trace and write to show the subtraction sentence for the set.

Count and Write 13 and 14

COMMON CORE STANDARD—K.CC.3
Know number names and the count sequence.

 1

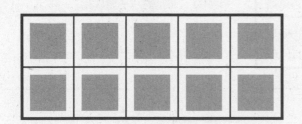 

_____
- - - - - - -
_____

 2

_____   _____   _____
- - - - - -  - - - - - -
_____   _____   _____

 3

_____
- - - - - - -
_____

4

_____   _____   _____
- - - - - -  - - - - - -
_____   _____   _____

DIRECTIONS   1. Count and tell how many. Write the number.   **2.** Look at the ten ones and some more ones in Exercise 1. Complete the addition sentence to match.   **3.** Count and tell how many. Write the number.   **4.** Look at the ten ones and some more ones in Exercise 3. Complete the addition sentence to match.

© Houghton Mifflin Harcourt Publishing Company

Lesson Check (K.CC.3)

 1

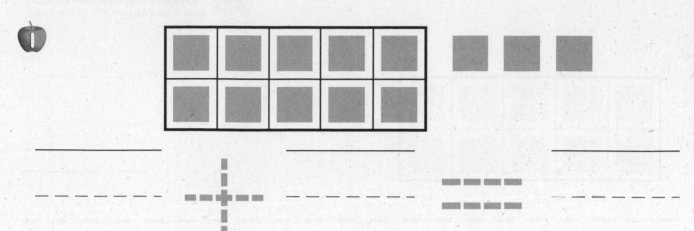

_____   +   _____   =   _____

Spiral Review (K.CC.4c, K.OA.1)

 2

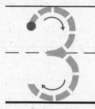 3 -- 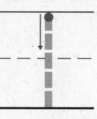 = _____

3

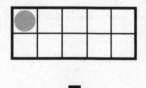

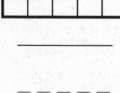 1 ___  3 4 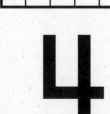 ___

DIRECTIONS **1.** Look at the ten ones and some more ones. Complete the addition sentence to match. **2.** Tell a subtraction word problem about the cats. Write and trace to complete the subtraction sentence. **3.** Count the dots in the ten frames. Begin with 1. Write the numbers in order as you count forward.

Model, Count, and Write 15

 COMMON CORE STANDARD—K.NBT.1
*Work with numbers 11–19 to gain
foundations for place value.*

 1

15
fifteen

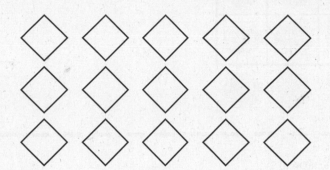

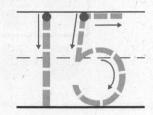

 2

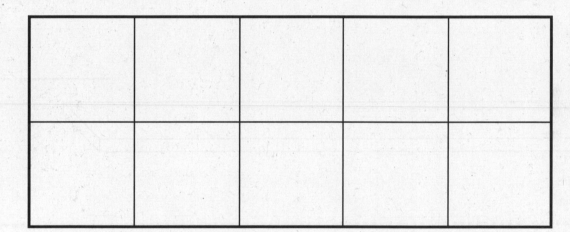

 3

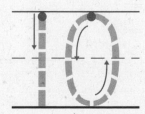 _____ **ones and** _____ **ones**

DIRECTIONS **1.** Count and tell how many. Trace the number. **2.** Use counters to
show the number 15. Draw the counters. **3.** Look at the counters you drew. How many
ones are in the ten frame? Trace the number. How many more ones? Write the number.

Lesson Check (K.NBT.1)

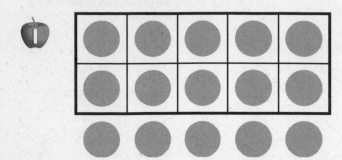

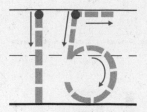

Spiral Review (K.CC.6, K.OA.5)

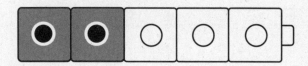

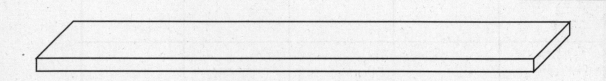

DIRECTIONS 1. Count and tell how many. Trace the number. 2. Draw to solve this problem. The number of plates on the shelf is two less than 8. How many plates are on the shelf? Draw the plates. Write the number. 3. Complete the addition sentence to show the numbers that match the cube train.

Problem Solving • Use Numbers to 15

 COMMON CORE STANDARD—K.CC.3
Know number names and the count sequence.

_____

_ _ _ _ _

_____ **carrot plants**

DIRECTIONS There are 15 vegetables in the garden. They are planted in rows of 5. There are 2 carrot plants and 3 potato plants in each row. How many carrot plants are in the garden? Draw to solve the problem.

_____
_ _ _ _ _
_____ **caps**

Spiral Review (K.OA.2, K.OA.4)

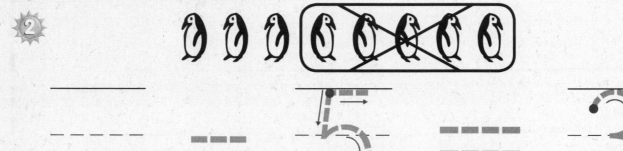

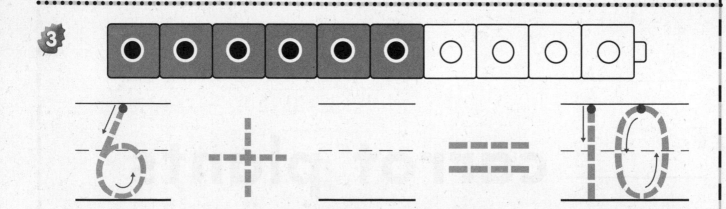

DIRECTIONS 1. There are 15 children. Ten children are each wearing 1 cap. How many more caps would you need to have one cap on each child?. Draw to solve the problem. Write how many more caps. **2.** Trace and write to show the subtraction sentence for the penguins. **3.** Look at the cube train. How many white cubes are added to the gray cubes to make 10? Write and trace to show this as an addition sentence.

Name _____

Model and Count 16 and 17

 COMMON CORE STANDARD—K.NBT.1
Work with numbers 11–19 to gain foundations for place value.

 17
seventeen

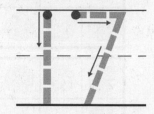

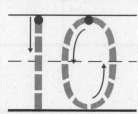 **ones and** _____ **ones**

DIRECTIONS **1.** Count and tell how many. Trace the number. **2.** Place counters in the ten frames to show the number 17. Draw the counters. **3.** Look at the counters you drew in the ten frames. How many ones are in the top ten frame? Trace the number. How many ones are in the bottom ten frame? Write the number.

Chapter 7

Lesson Check (K.NBT.1)

 ❶

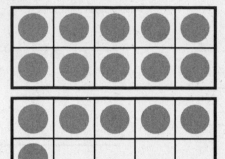

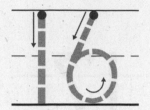

Spiral Review (K.CC.4b, K.OA.1)

❷

 2 + _____ == 3

❸

 5

DIRECTIONS **I.** Count and tell how many. Trace the number. **2.** Tell an addition word problem about the dogs. Write and trace to complete the addition sentence. **3.** How many counters would you place in the five frame to show the number? Draw the counters.

P128 one hundred twenty-eight

Name _____

Count and Write 16 and 17

COMMON CORE STANDARD—K.CC.3
Know number names and the count sequence.

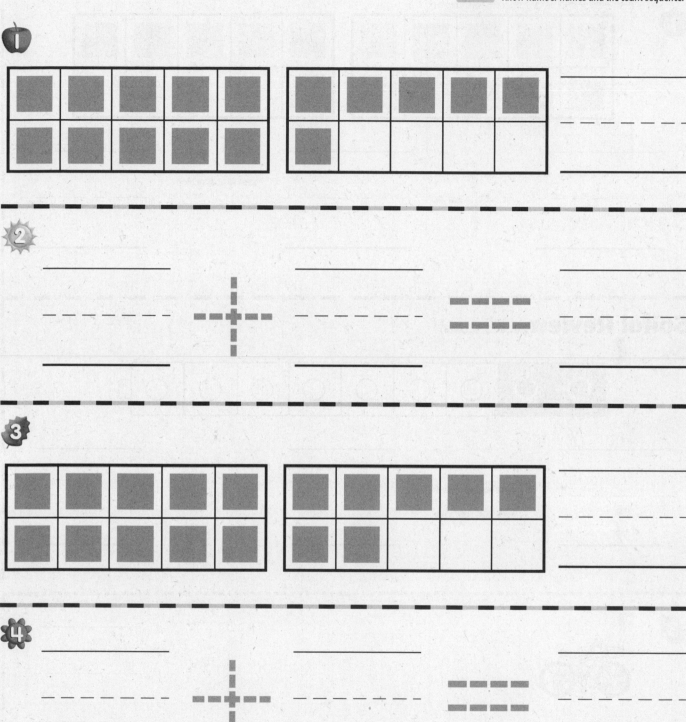

1

2 _____ + _____ = _____

3

4 _____ + _____ = _____

DIRECTIONS 1. Count and tell how many. Write the number. 2. Look at the ten frames in Exercise 1. Complete the addition sentence to match. 3. Count and tell how many. Write the number. 4. Look at the ten frames in Exercise 3. Complete the addition sentence to match.

Chapter 7

Lesson Check (K.CC.3)

 1

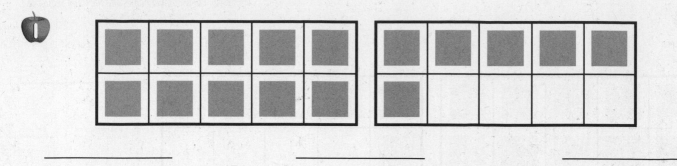

_____   _____   _____

- - - - - - + - - - - - - - - = = = - - - - - - - -

_____   _____   _____

Spiral Review (K.CC.3, K.OA.3)

2

_____   = = = _____   + _____

_____   _____   _____

3

_____

- - - - - - - - -

_____

DIRECTIONS 1. Look at the ten frames. Complete the addition sentence to match. **2.** Complete the addition sentence to show the numbers that match the cube train. **3.** How many bicycles are there? Write the number.

Model and Count 18 and 19

 COMMON CORE STANDARD—K.NBT.1
*Work with numbers 11–19 to gain
foundations for place value.*

 1

19
nineteen

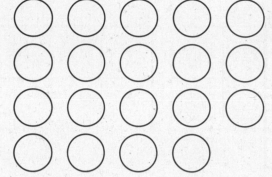

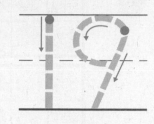

2

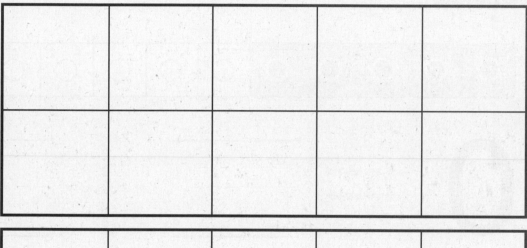

3

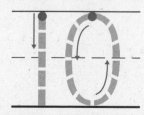 _____ **ones and** _____ **ones**

DIRECTIONS **1.** Count and tell how many. Trace the number. **2.** Place counters in the ten frame to show the number 19. Draw the counters. **3.** Look at the counters you drew in the ten frames. How many ones are in the top ten frame? Trace the number. How many ones are in the bottom ten frame? Write the numbers.

Chapter 7

Lesson Check (K.NBT.1)

 1

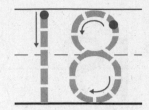

Spiral Review (K.OA.1, K.OA.3)

2

 **10** = ___ ___ + ___

3

 **4 take away 2**

_____

_ _ _ _ _ _

_____

DIRECTIONS **1.** Count and tell how many. Trace the number.   **2.** Complete the addition sentence to show the numbers that match the cube train.   **3.** Tell a subtraction word problem about the birds. Write the number that shows how many birds are left.

P132 one hundred thirty-two

Count and Write 18 and 19

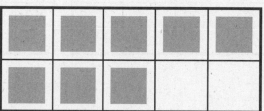

COMMON CORE STANDARD—K.CC.3
Know number names and the count sequence.

1

_____

2 _____ ___ + ___ ___ = ___ _____

3

_____

4 _____ ___ + ___ ___ = ___ _____

DIRECTIONS 1. Count and tell how many. Write the number. 2. Look at the ten frames in Exercise I. Complete the addition sentence to match. 3. Count and tell how many. Write the number. 4. Look at the ten frames in Exercise 3. Complete the addition sentence to match.

Lesson Check (K.CC.3)

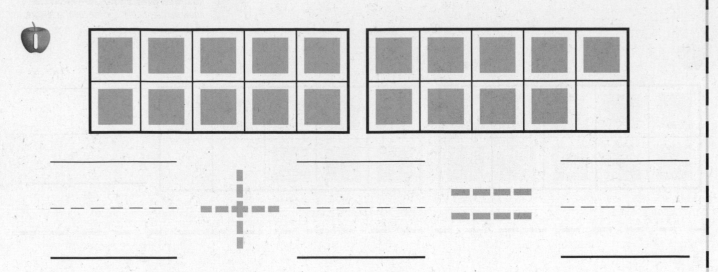

❶

_____ _____   ___ ___ _____

_____ _____

Spiral Review (K.CC.3, K.CC.5)

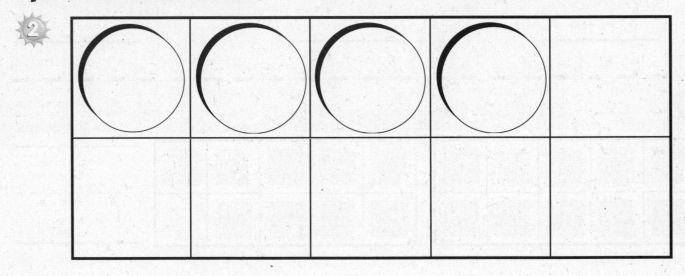

❷

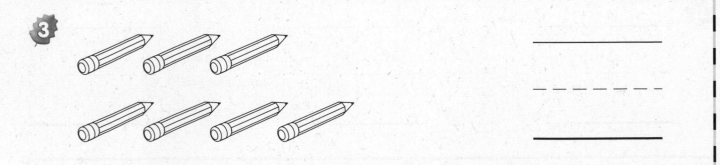

❸

_____

_ _ _ _ _ _ _ _ _

_____

DIRECTIONS 1. Look at the ten frames. Complete the addition sentence to match. 2. How many more counters would you place to model a way to make 8? Draw the counters. 3. How many pencils are there? Write the number.

School-Home
Letter

Dear Family,

My class started Chapter 8 this week. In this chapter, I will learn how to show, count, and write numbers to 20 and beyond.

Love, _____

Vocabulary

twenty I ten and 10 ones

🍎 🍎 🍎 🍎 🍎 🍎 🍎 🍎 🍎 🍎
🍎 🍎 🍎 🍎 🍎 🍎 🍎 🍎 🍎 🍎

20

Home Activity

Make a set of number flash cards. Ask your child to lay out 20 cards to model what a set of 20 objects looks like. Then ask your child to place the number cards in the correct order from I to 20. Have your child point to each card and count forward from the number I.

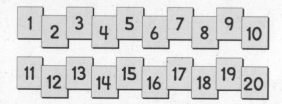

Literature

Look for these books at the library. Your child will enjoy these fun books while continuing to build counting skills.

20 Hungry Piggies by Trudy Harris. Millbrook Press, 2006.

Count! by Denise Fleming. Henry Holt and Co., 1995.

Carta
para la casa

Querida familia:

Mi clase comenzó el Capítulo 8 esta semana. En este capítulo, aprenderé cómo mostrar, contar y escribir números hasta el 20 y más allá. .

Con cariño, _____

Vocabulario

veinte una decena y 10 unidades

🍎 🍎 🍎 🍎 🍎 🍎 🍎 🍎 🍎 🍎
🍎 🍎 🍎 🍎 🍎 🍎 🍎 🍎 🍎 🍎

| 20 |

Actividad para la casa

Tome un conjunto de tarjetas nemotécnicas con números. Pídale a su hijo que separe 20 tarjetas para mostrar cómo es un conjunto de 20. Luego, pídale que ponga las tarjetas en el orden correcto del 1 al 20. Pídale a su hijo que señale cada carta y que cuente hacia delante desde el número 1.

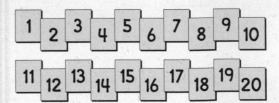

Literatura

Busque estos libros en la biblioteca. Su hijo disfrutará de estos libros divertidos mientras continua construir las habilidades de recuento.

20 Hungry Piggies por Trudy Harris. Millbrook Press, 2006.

Count! por Denise Fleming. Henry Holt and Co., 1995.

Model and Count 20

COMMON CORE STANDARD—K.CC.5
Count to tell the number of objects.

 1

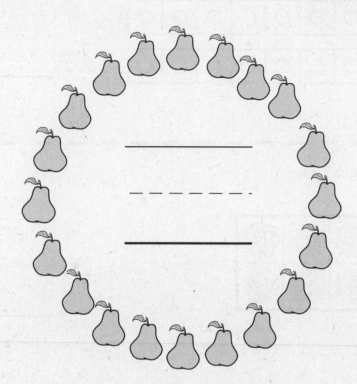

_____

- - - - - - - - - -

_____

 2

_____

- - - - - - - - - -

_____

DIRECTIONS 1–2. Count and tell how many pieces of fruit. Write the number. Tell a friend how you counted the fruit.

Chapter 8

Lesson Check (K.CC.5)

_____

- - - - - - - - - - - -

_____

Spiral Review (K.OA.5, K.NBT.1)

_____

- - - - - - - - - - - -

_____

      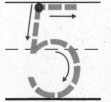

DIRECTIONS   1–2. Count and tell how many. Write the number.   3. Tell an addition word problem about the boats. Write and trace to complete the addition sentence.

Count and Write to 20

COMMON CORE STANDARD—K.CC.3
Know number names and the count sequence.

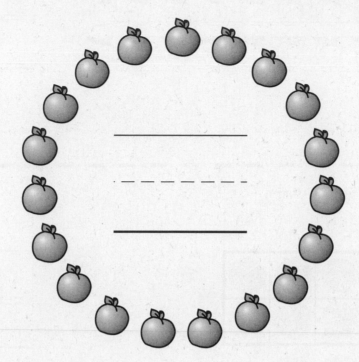

_____

- - - - - - -

_____

- -

_____

- - - - - - -

_____

DIRECTIONS **1–2.** Count and tell how many pieces of fruit. Write the number.

Lesson Check (K.CC.3)

_____

- - - - - - - - - - - -

_____

Spiral Review (K.OA.5, K.NBT.1)

_____

- - - - - - - - - - - -

_____

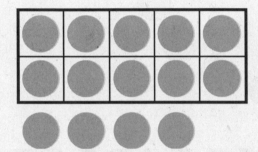

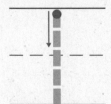  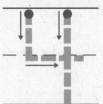

_____

_____

DIRECTIONS 1–2. Count and tell how many. Write the number. **3.** Complete the addition sentence to show the numbers that match the cube train.

Count and Order to 20

1.

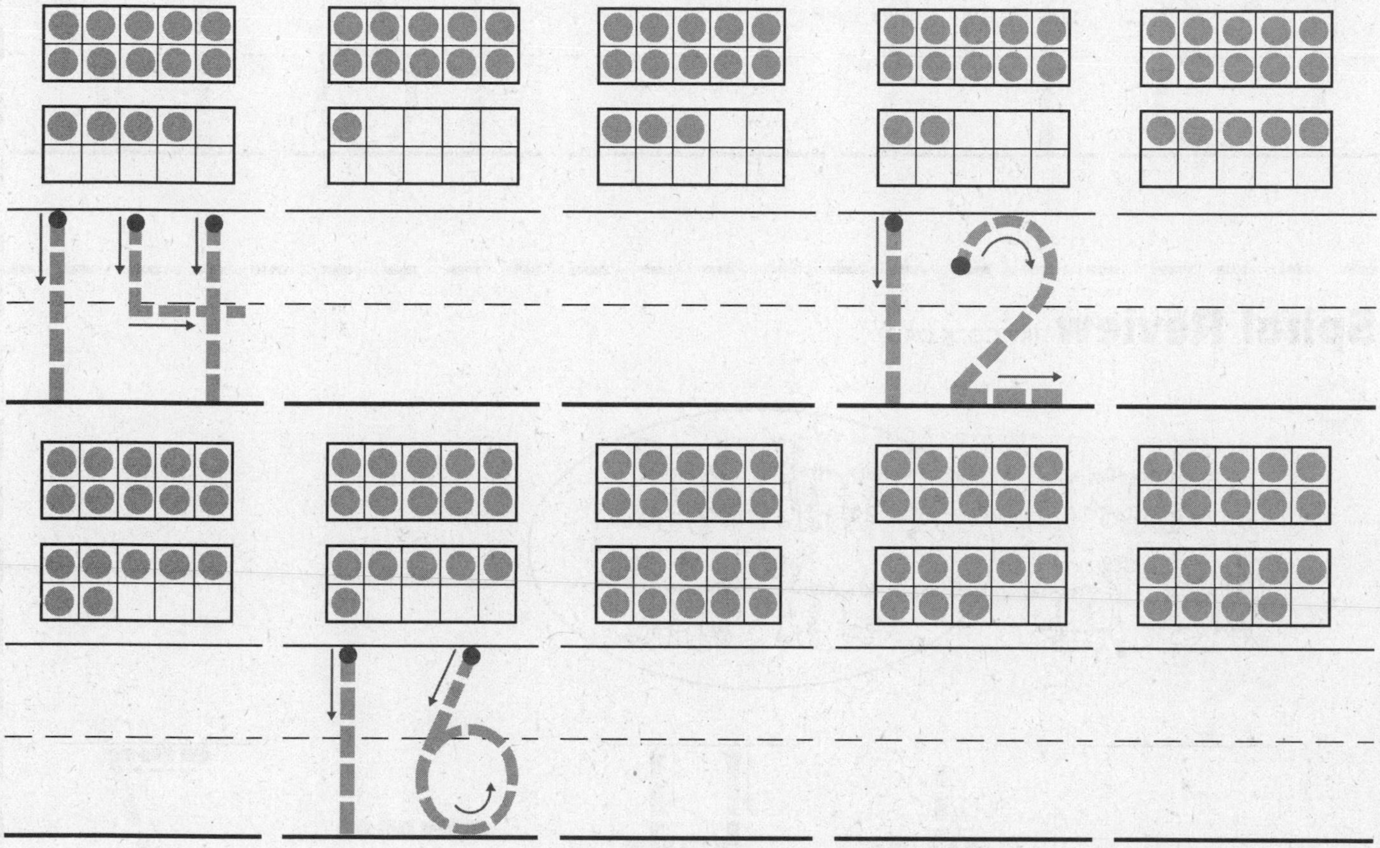

2.

© Houghton Mifflin Harcourt Publishing Company

DIRECTIONS 1. Count the dots in each set of ten frames. Trace or write the numbers. 2. Trace and write those numbers in order.

Lesson Check (K.CC.2)

1

13 14   16 17

Spiral Review (K.CC.3, K.OA.2)

2

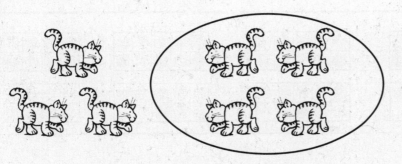

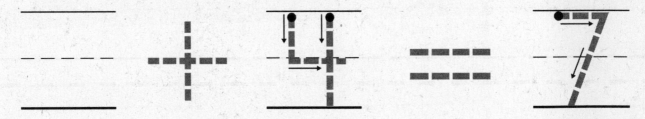
___ + 4 === 7

3

___

- - -

___

DIRECTIONS 1. Count forward. Trace and write the numbers in order. **2.** Tell an addition word problem about the cats. Write and trace to complete the addition sentence. **3.** How many erasers are there? Write the number.

Name _____

Problem Solving • Compare Numbers to 20

COMMON CORE STANDARD—K.CC.6
Compare numbers.

DIRECTIONS   **1.** Teni has 16 berries. She has a number of berries two greater than Marta. Use cubes to model the sets of berries. Compare the sets. Which set is larger? Draw the cubes. Write how many in each set. Circle the greater number. Tell a friend how you compared the numbers.   **2.** Ben has 18 pears. Sophia has a number of pears two less than Ben. Use cubes to model the sets of pears. Compare the sets. Which set is smaller? Draw the cubes. Write how many in each set. Circle the number that is less. Tell a friend how you compared the numbers.

Lesson Check (K.CC.6)

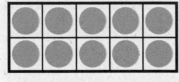

_____

- - - - - - - - -

_____

_____

- - - - - - - - -

_____

Spiral Review (K.CC.6, K.NBT.1)

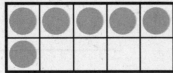

_____

- - - - - - - - -

_____

DIRECTIONS I. Jim has 20 grapes. Mia has a number of grapes two less than Jim. Use cubes to model the sets of grapes. Compare the sets. Which set is smaller? Draw the cubes. Write how many in each set. Circle the number that is less.   2. Count and tell how many. Write the number.   3. Count the counters in each set. Circle the set that has a greater number of counters.

Count to 50 by Ones

COMMON CORE STANDARD—K.CC.1
Know number names and the count sequence.

1	2	3	4	5	6	7	8	9	10
11	12	13	14	15	16	17	18	19	20
21	22	23	24	25	26	27	28	29	30
31	32	33	34	35	36	37	38	39	40
41	42	43	44	45	46	47	48	49	50

DIRECTIONS **1.** Look away and point to any number. Circle that number. Count forward from that number. Draw a line under the number 50.

Lesson Check (K.CC.1)

1	2	3	4	5	6	7	8	9	10
11	12	13	14	15	16	17	18	19	20
21	22	23	24	25	26	27	28	29	30

Spiral Review (K.OA.1, K.OA.3)

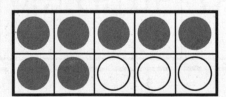 $10 - 3 =$ _____

DIRECTIONS **1.** Begin with 1 and count forward to 20. What is the next number? Draw a line under that number. **2.** Complete the addition sentence to show the numbers that match the cube train. **3.** Shelley has 10 counters. Three of her counters are white. The rest of her counters are gray. How many are gray? Complete the subtraction sentence to show the answer. (Lesson 6.2)

P146 one hundred forty-six

© Houghton Mifflin Harcourt Publishing Company

Name _____

Count to 100 by Ones

COMMON CORE STANDARD—K.CC.1
Know number names and the count sequence.

1	2	3	4	5	6	7	8	9	10
11	12	13	14	15	16	17	18	19	20
21	22	23	24	25	26	27	28	29	30
31	32	33	34	35	36	37	38	39	40
41	42	43	44	45	46	47	48	49	50
51	52	53	54	55	56	57	58	59	60
61	62	63	64	65	66	67	68	69	70
71	72	73	74	75	76	77	78	79	80
81	82	83	84	85	86	87	88	89	90
91	92	93	94	95	96	97	98	99	100

DIRECTIONS 1. Point to each number as you count to 100. Look away and point to any number. Circle that number. Count forward to 100 from that number. Draw a line under the number 100.

Lesson Check (K.CC.1)

🍎 1

71	72	73	74	75	76	77	78	79	80
81	82	83	84	85	86	87	88	89	90
91	92	93	94	95	96	97	98	99	100

Spiral Review (K.CC.6, K.OA.5)

2

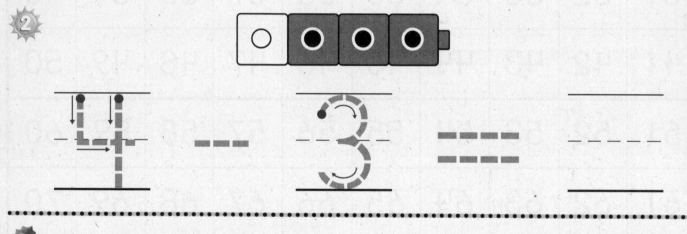

4 − 3 = _____

3

_____

_____

_____

_____

DIRECTIONS 1. Begin with 71 and count forward to 80. What is the next number? Draw a line under that number. 2. Pete makes the cube train shown. He takes the cube train apart to show how many cubes are gray. Complete the subtraction sentence to show Pete's cube train. 3. Count how many flowers. Write the number. Draw to show a set of counters that has the same number as the set of flowers. Write the number.

Count to 100 by Tens

COMMON CORE STANDARD—K.CC.1
Know number names and the count sequence.

51	52	53	54	55	56	57	58	59	60
61	62	63	64	65	66	67	68	69	70
71	72	73	74	75	76	77	78	79	80
81	82	83	84	85	86	87	88	89	90
91	92	93	94	95	96	97	98	99	100

DIRECTIONS I. Trace the numbers to complete the counting order to 100. Count by tens as you point to the numbers you traced.

© Houghton Mifflin Harcourt Publishing Company

Lesson Check (K.CC.1)

1

1	2	3	4	5	6	7	8	9	10
11	12	13	14	15	16	17	18	19	20
21	22	23	24	25	26	27	28	29	30

Spiral Review (K.CC.3, K.OA.5)

_____

_ _ _ _ _ _ _ _ _ _

_____

3

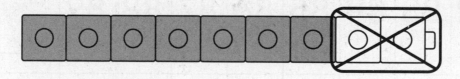

____   ____   ____   ▬▬▬   ____

____   --   _ _ _   ▬▬▬   _ _ _

____   ____   ____   ▬▬▬   ____

DIRECTIONS 1. Count by tens as you point to the numbers in the shaded boxes. Start with the number 10. What number do you end with? Draw a line under that number. 2. How many tiles are there? Write the number. 3. Complete the subtraction sentence that matches the cube train.

Name _____

Count by Tens

COMMON CORE STANDARD—K.CC.1
Know number names and the count sequence.

1

20   30   40

2

30   40   50

3

60   70   80

4

80   90   100

5

80   90   100

DIRECTIONS 1–5. Point to each set of 10 as you count by tens.
Circle the number that shows how many.

Chapter 8

Lesson Check (K.CC.1)

60   70   80

Spiral Review (K.OA.3, K.NBT.1)

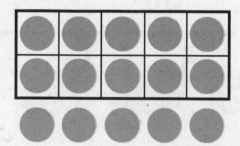

_____

- - - - - - - - - - -

_____

4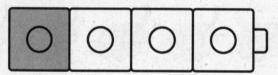

DIRECTIONS **1.** Point to each set of 10 as you count by tens. Circle the number that shows how many crayons there are. **2.** Count and tell how many. Write the number. **3.** Complete the addition sentence to match the cube train.

P152 one hundred fifty-two

School-Home Letter

Dear Family,

My class started Chapter 9 this week. In this chapter, I will learn how to identify, name, and describe two-dimensional shapes.

Love, _____

Vocabulary

curve a line that is rounded

vertex the point where two sides of a two-dimensional shape meet

vertex

Home Activity

Spread out a group of household objects. Have your child point out the objects that look like circles, squares, and triangles.

  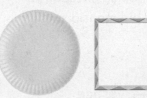

Literature

Look for these books at the library. The pictures will capture your child's imagination.

Shapes, Shapes, Shapes by Tana Hoban. Greenwillow, 1996.

Color Farm by Lois Ehlert. HarperCollins, 1990.

Carta
para la casa

Querida familia:

Mi clase comenzó el Capítulo 9 esta semana. En este capítulo, aprenderé cómo identiﬁcar, nombrar y describir ﬁguras bidimensionales.

Con cariño, _____

Vocabulario

curva una línea que no es recta

vértice el punto en donde se encuentran dos lados de una figura bidimensional

Actividad para la casa

Dé a su hijo varios objetos que encuentre en la casa y pídale que señale los que se parezcan a los cuadrados, círculos y triángulos.

Literatura

Busque este libro en la biblioteca. Las ilustraciones estimularán la imaginación de su hijo.

Shapes, Shapes, Shapes
por Tana Hoban. Greenwillow, 1996.

Color Farm
por Lois Ehlert. HarperCollins, 1990.

Name _____

Identify and Name Circles

COMMON CORE STANDARD—K.G.2
Identify and describe shapes (squares, circles, triangles, rectangles, hexagons, cubes, cones, cylinders, and spheres).

DIRECTIONS 1. Color the circles in the picture.

Chapter 9

one hundred fifty-five **P155**

Lesson Check (K.G.2)

 1

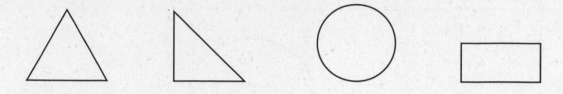

Spiral Review (K.CC.2, K.OA.2)

 2

 3

$$\underline{} + 3 = 8$$

DIRECTIONS 1. Color the circle.   2. Count forward. Trace and write the numbers in order.   3. Which number completes the addition sentence about the sets of cats? Write the number.

Name _____

Describe Circles

 COMMON CORE STANDARD—K.G.4
Analyze, compare, create, and compose shapes.

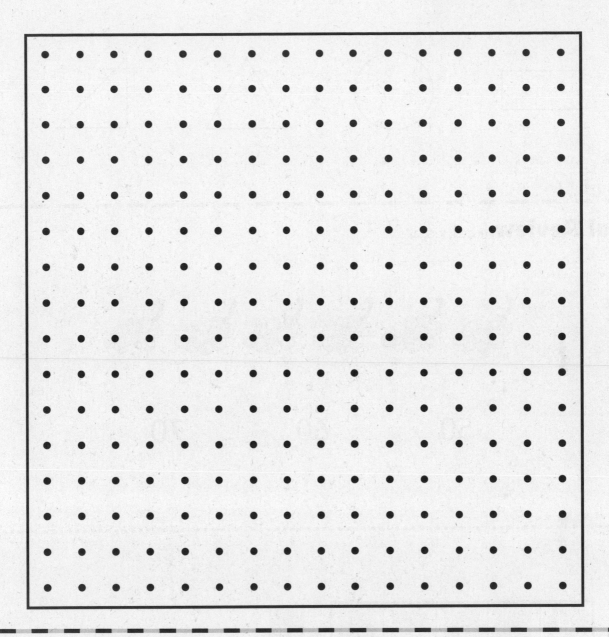

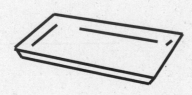 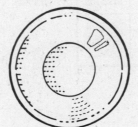 

DIRECTIONS **I.** Use a pencil to hold one end of a large paper clip on one of the dots in the center. Place another pencil in the other end of the paper clip. Move the pencil around to draw a circle. **2.** Color the object that is shaped like a circle.

Chapter 9   one hundred fifty-seven   P157

Spiral Review (K.CC.1, K.CC.3)

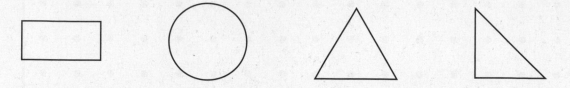

50   60   70

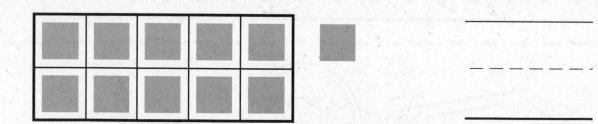

DIRECTIONS 1. Which shape has a curve? Color that shape. 2. Point to each set of 10 as you count by tens. Circle the number that shows how many grapes there are. 3. How many tiles are there? Write the number.

Identify and Name Squares

COMMON CORE STANDARD—K.G.2
Identify and describe shapes (squares, circles, triangles, rectangles, hexagons, cubes, cones, cylinders, and spheres).

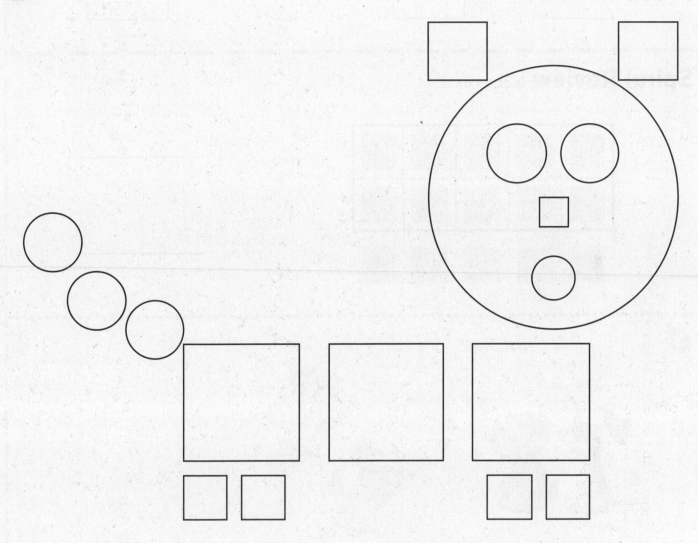

DIRECTIONS I. Color the squares in the picture.

Spiral Review (K.CC.3, K.OA.1)

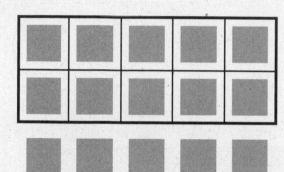

_____

– – – – – – – – –

_____

 and 2 _____

DIRECTIONS 1. Which shape is a square? Color the square. 2. How many tiles are there? Write the number. 3. Trace the number of puppies. Trace the number of puppies being added. Write the number that shows how many puppies there are now.

Describe Squares

COMMON CORE STANDARD—K.G.4
Analyze, compare, create, and compose shapes.

 1

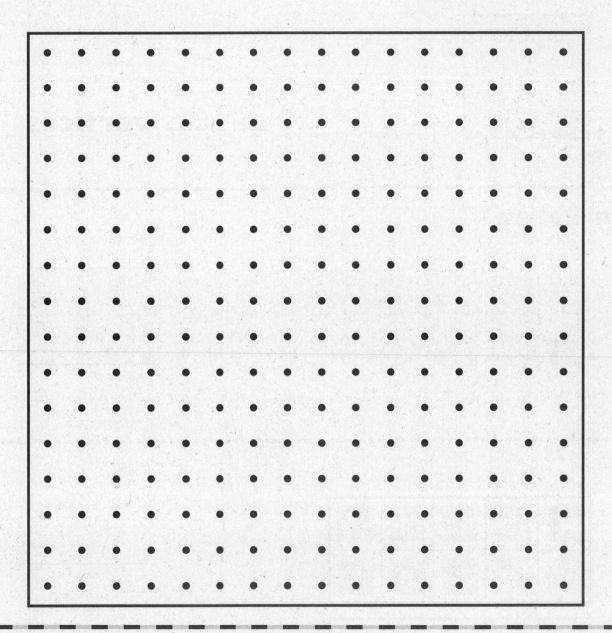

2 _____

3 _____

_____ **vertices**   _____ **sides**

DIRECTIONS 1. Draw and color a square. 2. Place a counter on each corner, or vertex, of the square that you drew. Write how many corners, or vertices. 3. Trace around the sides of the square that you drew. Write how many sides.

Lesson Check (K.G.4)

1

_____

\- \- \- \- \-

_____ **vertices**

Spiral Review (K.CC.3)

2

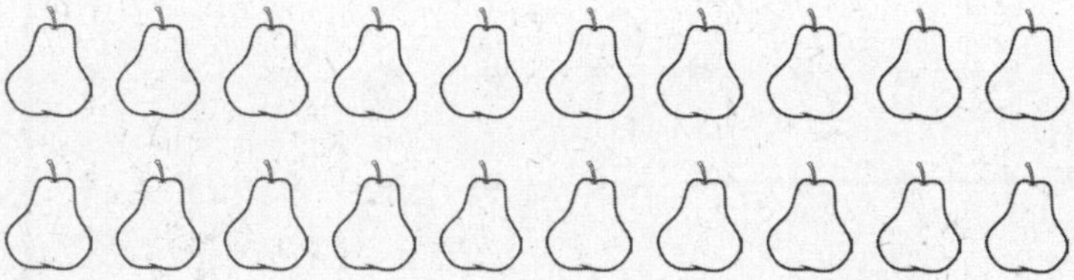

_____

\- \- \- \- \-

_____

3

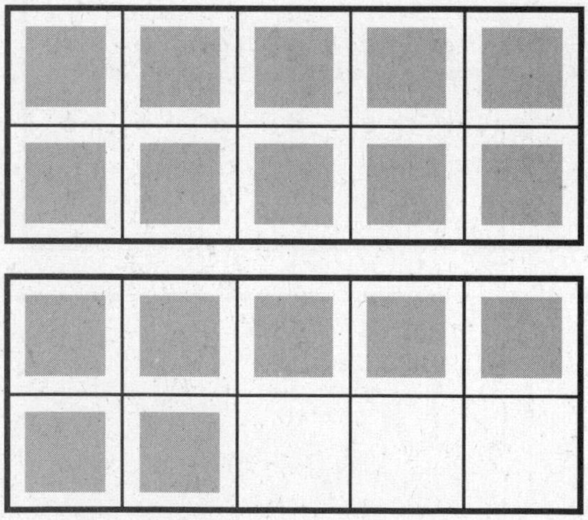

_____

\- \- \- \- \-

_____

DIRECTIONS 1. How many vertices does the square have? Write the number. 2. Count and tell how many pieces of fruit. Write the number. 3. How many tiles are there? Write the number.

Identify and Name Triangles

COMMON CORE STANDARD—K.G.2
Identify and describe shapes (squares, circles, triangles, rectangles, hexagons, cubes, cones, cylinders, and spheres).

DIRECTIONS 1–2. Color the triangles in the picture.

Lesson Check (K.G.2)

Spiral Review (K.CC.1, K.CC.5)

1	2	3	4	5	6	7	8	9	10
11	12	13	14	15	16	17	18	19	20
21	22	23	24	25	26	27	28	29	30

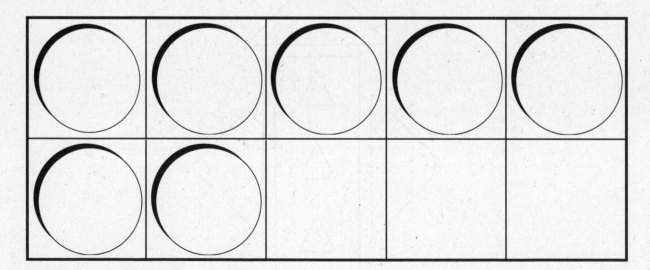

DIRECTIONS **1.** Which shape is a triangle? Color the triangle. **2.** Begin with 1 and count forward to 24. What is the next number? Draw a line under that number. **3.** How many more counters would you place to model a way to make 10? Draw the counters.

Describe Triangles

COMMON CORE STANDARD—K.G.4
Analyze, compare, create, and compose shapes.

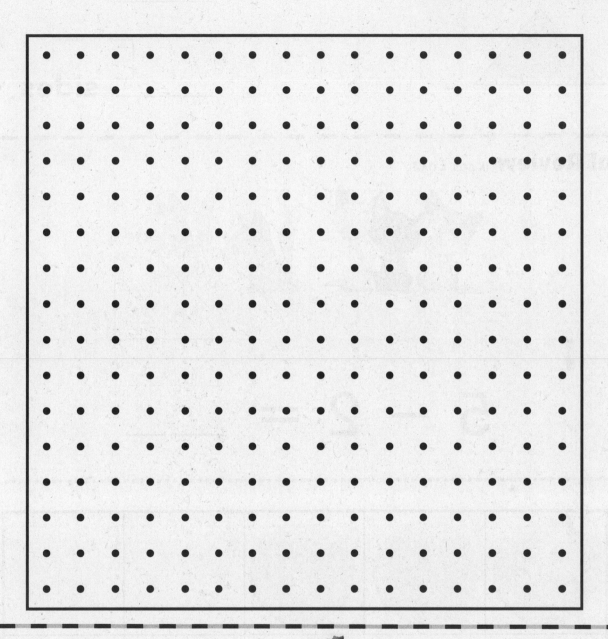

2 _____ **vertices**

3 _____ **sides**

DIRECTIONS 1. Draw and color a triangle. 2. Place a counter on each corner, or vertex, of the triangle that you drew. Write how many corners, or vertices. 3. Trace around the sides of the triangle that you drew. Write how many sides.

Chapter 9

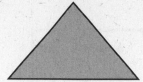

_____

- - - - - - -

_____ **sides**

Spiral Review (K.CC.5, K.OA.1)

$$5 - 2 = \underline{\quad\quad}$$

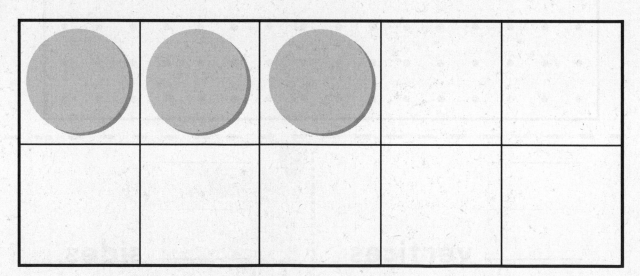

DIRECTIONS 1. How many sides does the triangle have? Write the number. **2.** Which number shows how many kittens are left? Write the number. **3.** How many more counters would you place to model a way to make 7? Draw the counters.

Identify and Name Rectangles

COMMON CORE STANDARD—K.G.2
Identify and describe shapes (squares, circles, triangles, rectangles, hexagons, cubes, cones, cylinders, and spheres).

DIRECTIONS 1. Color the rectangles in the picture.

Lesson Check (K.G.2)

Spiral Review (K.CC.1, K.CC.5)

1	2	3	4	5	6	7	8	9	10
11	12	13	14	15	16	17	18	19	20
21	22	23	24	25	26	27	28	29	30

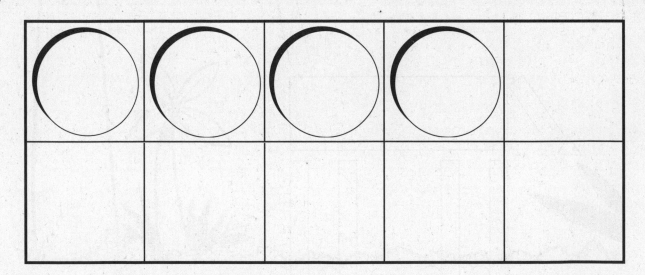

DIRECTIONS **1.** Which shape is a rectangle? Color the rectangle.
2. Count by tens as you point to the numbers in the shaded boxes. Start
with the number 10. What number do you end with? Draw a line under
that number. **3.** How many more counters would you place to model a
way to make 6? Draw the counters.

P168 one hundred sixty-eight

Describe Rectangles

 **COMMON CORE STANDARD—K.G.4**
Analyze, compare, create, and compose shapes.

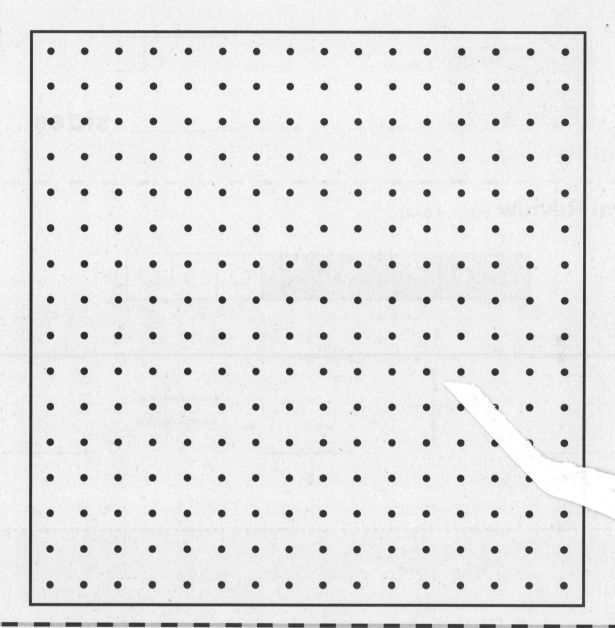

---

2 _____
_ _ _ _ _ _
_____ **vertices**

3 _____
_ _ _ _ _ _
_____ **sides**

DIRECTIONS I. Draw and color a rectangle. 2. Place a
counter on each corner, or vertex, of the rectangle that you drew.
Write how many corners, or vertices. 3. Trace around the sides
of the rectangle that you drew. Write how many sides.

1

_____

- - - - -

_____ **sides**

Spiral Review (K.CC.6, K.OA.2)

2

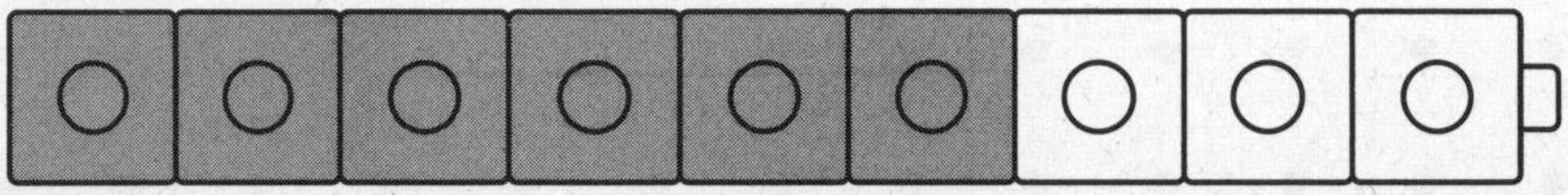

_____   \+   _____   =   _____

3

_____

- - - - -

_____

DIRECTIONS   I. How many sides does the rectangle have? Write the number.   **2.** Complete the addition sentence to show the numbers that match the cube train.   **3.** Draw a set that has a number of cubes two greater than 18. Write the number.

Identify and Name Hexagons

COMMON CORE STANDARD—K.G.2
Identify and describe shapes (squares, circles, triangles, rectangles, hexagons, cubes, cones, cylinders, and spheres).

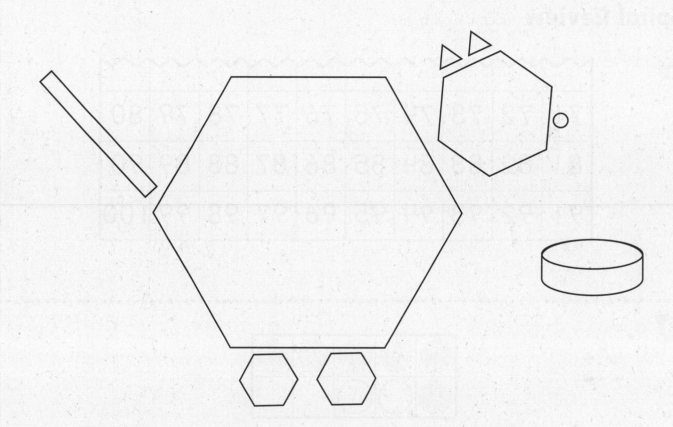

DIRECTIONS **1.** Color the hexagons in the picture.

Lesson Check (K.G.2)

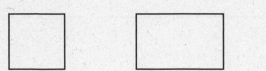

Spiral Review (K.CC.1, K.OA.1)

71	72	73	74	75	76	77	78	79	80
81	82	83	84	85	86	87	88	89	90
91	92	93	94	95	96	97	98	99	100

3

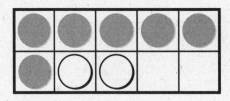

_____   _____

 +

_____   _____

DIRECTIONS 1. Which shape is a hexagon? Color the hexagon.
2. Begin with 81 and count forward to 90. What is the next number?
Draw a line under that number. 3. What numbers show the sets that
are put together? Write the numbers and trace the symbol.

P172 one hundred seventy-two

Describe Hexagons

COMMON CORE STANDARD—K.G.4
Analyze, compare, create, and compose shapes.

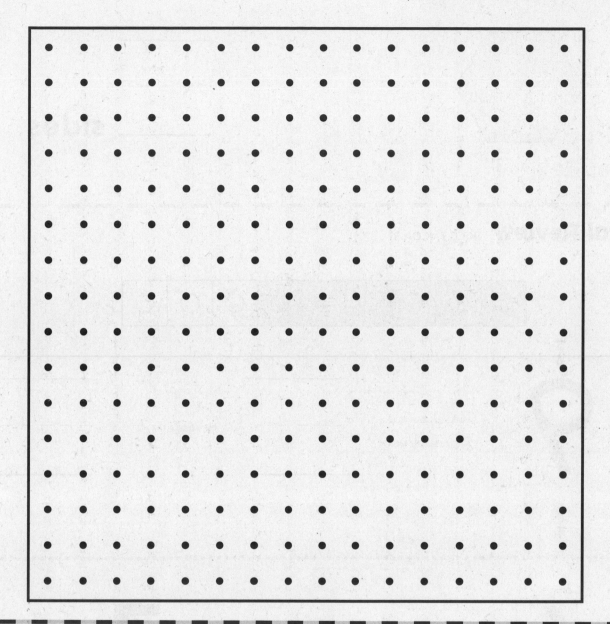

2 _____

_____ **vertices**

3 _____

_____ **sides**

DIRECTIONS **1.** Draw and color a hexagon. **2.** Place a counter on each corner, or vertex, of the hexagon that you drew. Write how many corners, or vertices. **3.** Trace around the sides of the hexagon that you drew. Write how many sides.

Lesson Check (K.G.4)

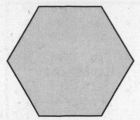

_____

_ _ _ _ _

_____ sides

Spiral Review (K.CC.7, K.OA.3)

$$9 = \text{\_\_\_\_} + \text{\_\_\_\_}$$

---

6   7

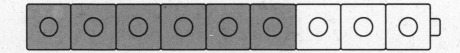

DIRECTIONS   1. How many sides does the hexagon have? Write the number.   **2.** Complete the addition sentence to show the numbers that match the cube train.   **3.** Compare the numbers. Circle the number that is greater.

P174 one hundred seventy-four

Name _____

Algebra • Compare Two-Dimensional Shapes

COMMON CORE STANDARD—K.G.4
Analyze, compare, create, and compose shapes.

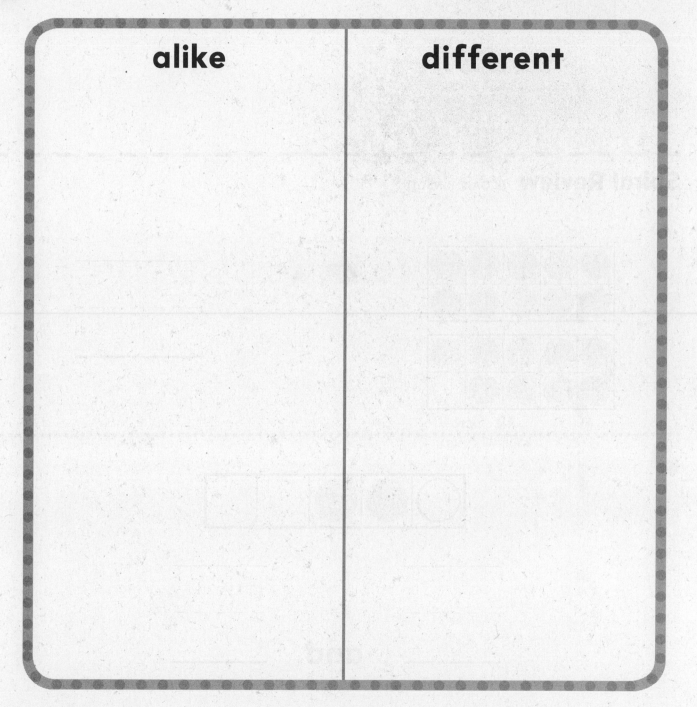

alike	different

DIRECTIONS **I.** Place two-dimensional shapes on the page. Sort the shapes by the number of sides. Draw the shapes on the sorting mat. Use the words *alike* and *different* to tell how you sorted the shapes.

Chapter 9

Lesson Check (K.G.4)

Spiral Review (K.OA.1, K.NBT.1)

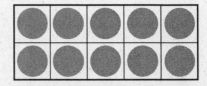

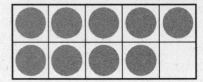

_____

_ _ _ _ _ _ _ _ _

_____

_____   _____

_ _ _ _ _ _ _   _ _ _ _ _ _ _

_____ **and** _____

DIRECTIONS 1. Look at the shape. Draw a shape that is alike in some way. Tell how the two shapes are alike. **2.** Count and tell how many. Write the number. **3.** How many of each color counter? Write the numbers.

P176 one hundred seventy-six

Problem Solving • Draw to Join Shapes

COMMON CORE STANDARD—K.G.6
Analyze, compare, create, and compose shapes.

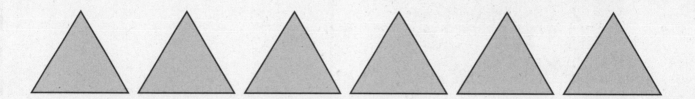

 1.

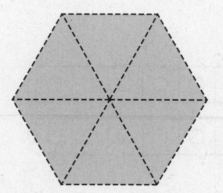

 2.

DIRECTIONS **1.** Place triangles on the page as shown. How can you join all of the triangles to make a hexagon? Trace around the triangles to draw the hexagon. **2.** How can you join some of the triangles to make a larger triangle? Trace around the triangles to draw the larger triangle.

Chapter 9

Lesson Check (K.G.6)

Spiral Review (K.CC.5, K.CC.6)

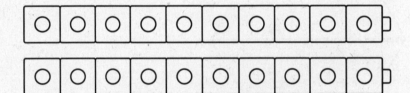

_____

- - - - - - - - - - - - -

_____

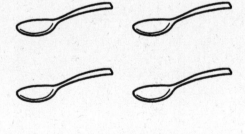

_____   _____

- - - - - - - - -   - - - - - - - - -

_____   _____

DIRECTIONS I. Join two triangles to make the shape. Draw and color the triangles you used. **2.** Count and tell how many. Write the number. **3.** Count and tell how many in each set. Write the numbers. Compare the numbers. Circle the number that is less.

School-Home
Letter

Dear Family,

My class started Chapter 10 this week. In this chapter, I will learn how identifying and describing shapes can help me sort them.

Love, _____

Vocabulary

sphere a three-dimensional shape that is round
A ball is an example of a sphere.

cylinder a three-dimensional shape with a curved surface and two flat surfaces

Home Activity

Take a walk around your neighborhood with your child. Ask your child to point out objects that are shaped like three-dimensional shapes, such as spheres, cubes, cylinders, and cones.

Recycle

Literature

Look for these books at the library. The pictures will help your child understand how shapes are a part of everyday life.

What in the World Is a Sphere?
by Anders Hanson. SandCastle, 2007.

Cubes, Cones, Cylinders, & Spheres
by Tana Hoban. Greenwillow Books, 2000.

Carta
para la casa

Querida familia:

Mi clase comenzó el Capítulo 10 esta semana. En este capítulo, aprenderé cómo identificar y describir figuras puede ayudarme a clasificarlas.

Con cariño, _____

Vocabulario

esfera una figura tridimensional redonda

Una pelota es un ejemplo de esfera.

cilindro una figura tridimensional con una superficie curva y dos superficies planas

Actividad para la casa

Salga a caminar por el barrio junto a su hijo. Pídale que señale objetos que tengan formas tridimensionales, tales como esferas, cubos, cilindros y conos.

Literatura

Busque estos libros en la biblioteca. Los dibujos ayudarán a que su hijo comprenda cómo las figuras forman parte de la vida diaria.

What in the World Is a Sphere?
por Anders Hanson. SandCastle, 2007.

Cubes, Cones, Cylinders & Spheres
por Tana Hoban. Greenwillow Books, 2000.

Three-Dimensional Shapes

COMMON CORE STANDARD—K.G.4
Analyze, compare, create, and compose shapes.

 roll

 stack

 slide

 **stack and slide**

DIRECTIONS 1. Which shape does not roll? Mark an X on that shape. 2. Which shapes do not stack? Mark an X on those shapes. 3. Which shape does not slide? Mark an X on that shape. 4. Which shape does not stack and slide? Mark an X on that shape.

Lesson Check (K.G.4)

Spiral Review (K.CC.2, K.G.4)

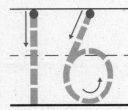 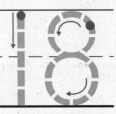

DIRECTIONS **1.** Which shape does not roll? Mark an X on the shape. **2.** Count forward. Trace and write the numbers in order. **3.** Which shape has a curve? Color the shape.

Identify, Name, and Describe Spheres

COMMON CORE STANDARD—K.G.2
Identify and describe shapes (squares, circles, triangles, rectangles, hexagons, cubes, cones, cylinders, and spheres).

DIRECTIONS I. Identify the objects that are shaped like a sphere. Mark an X on those objects.

Lesson Check (K.G.2)

Spiral Review (K.CC.3, K.G.2)

_____

- - - - - - - - - - - -

_____

DIRECTIONS **1.** Which shape is a sphere? Mark an X on the shape. **2.** Which shape is a square? Color the square. **3.** How many school buses are there? Write the number.

Identify, Name, and Describe Cubes

COMMON CORE STANDARD—K.G.2
Identify and describe shapes (squares, circles, triangles, rectangles, hexagons, cubes, cones, cylinders, and spheres).

DIRECTIONS 1. Identify the objects that are shaped like a cube. Mark an X on those objects.

Chapter 10

one hundred eighty-five **P185**

Lesson Check (K.G.2)

Spiral Review (K.CC.1, K.G.4)

_____

- - - - - - - - - - - -

_____ **sides**

71	72	73	74	75	76	77	78	79	80
81	82	83	84	85	86	87	88	89	90
91	92	93	94	95	96	97	98	99	100

DIRECTIONS 1. Which shape is a cube? Mark an X on the shape. 2. How many sides does the square have? Write the number. 3. Begin with 81 and count forward to 90. What is the next number? Draw a line under that number.

Identify, Name, and Describe Cylinders

COMMON CORE STANDARD—K.G.2
Identify and describe shapes (squares, circles, triangles, rectangles, hexagons, cubes, cones, cylinders, and spheres).

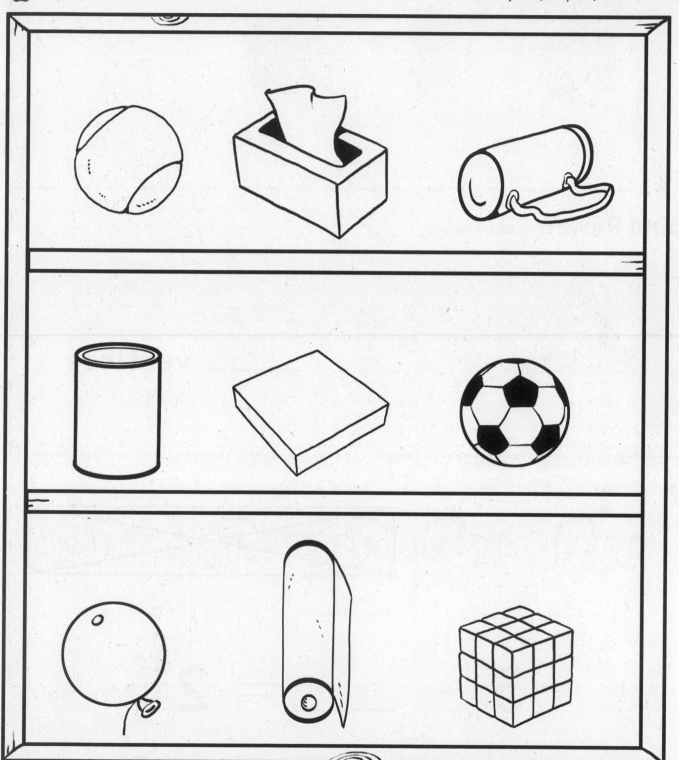

DIRECTIONS I. Identify the objects that are shaped like a cylinder. Mark an X on those objects.

Chapter 10

Lesson Check (K.G.2)

 ❶

Spiral Review (K.OA.5, K.G.4)

❷

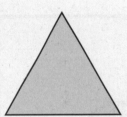

_____

- - - - - - -

_____ **vertices**

❸

_____

- - - - - -

$$5 - \underline{\quad} = 2$$

DIRECTIONS 1. Which shape is a cylinder? Mark an X on the shape. 2. How many vertices does the triangle have? Write the number. 3. Write the number to show how many are being taken from the set.

Identify, Name, and Describe Cones

 COMMON CORE STANDARD—K.G.2
Identify and describe shapes (squares, circles, triangles, rectangles, hexagons, cubes, cones, cylinders, and spheres).

DIRECTIONS 1. Identify the objects that are shaped like a cone. Mark an X on those objects.

Lesson Check (K.G.2)

Spiral Review (K.NBT.1, K.G.2)

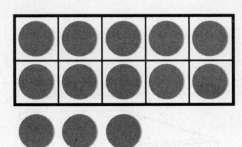

_____

- - - - - - - - - - -

_____

DIRECTIONS 1. Which shape is a cone? Mark an X on the shape. 2. Count and tell how many. Write the number. 3. Which shape is a circle? Color the circle.

Problem Solving • Two- and Three-Dimensional Shapes

COMMON CORE STANDARD—K.G.3
Identify and describe shapes (squares, circles, triangles, rectangles, hexagons, cubes, cones, cylinders, and spheres).

  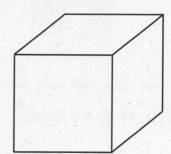

 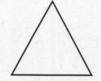

 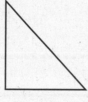 

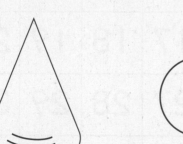 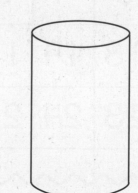 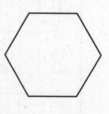

DIRECTIONS 1. Identify the two-dimensional or flat shapes. Use red to color the flat shapes. Identify the three-dimensional or solid shapes. Use blue to color the solid shapes.

Lesson Check (K.G.3)

   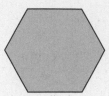

Spiral Review (K.CC.1, K.G.6)

1	2	3	4	5	6	7	8	9	10
11	12	13	14	15	16	17	18	19	20
21	22	23	24	25	26	27	28	29	30

DIRECTIONS 1. Which is a three-dimensional or solid shape? Mark an X on the shape. 2. Join two triangles to make the shape. Draw and color the triangles you used. 3. Begin with 1 and count forward to 19. What is the next number? Draw a line under that number.

Name _____

Model Shapes

COMMON CORE STANDARD—K.G.5
Model shapes in the world by building shapes from components (e.g., sticks and clay balls) and drawing shapes.

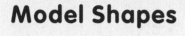

_____
- - - - - -
_____ **sides**

_____
- - - - - -
_____ **flat surfaces**

DIRECTIONS 1. Draw to show what you know about a square. Write how many sides. 2. Use clay to model a cylinder. How many flat surfaces are there?

Lesson Check (K.G.5)

_____

- - - - - - -

_____ **flat surfaces**

Spiral Review (K.G.2, K.OA.2)

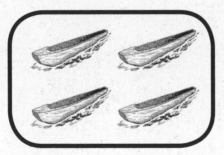

4 + ___ = 5

DIRECTIONS **1.** How many flat surfaces does this shape have? Write the number. **2.** Which shape is flat? Color the flat shape. **3.** Tell an addition word problem about the boats. Write the number to complete the addition sentence.

Name _____

Above and Below

COMMON CORE STANDARD—K.G.1
Identify and describe shapes (squares, circles, triangles, rectangles, hexagons, cubes, cones, cylinders, and spheres).

DIRECTIONS I. Mark an X on the object that is shaped like a sphere below the table. Circle the object that is shaped like a cube above the table.

Chapter 10

one hundred ninety-five **P195**

Lesson Check (K.G.1)

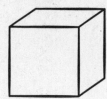

CAT TOYS

Spiral Review (K.CC.5, K.G.4)

⬜⬜⬜⬜⬜⬜⬜⬜⬜⬜

⬜⬜⬜⬜⬜⬜⬜⬜⬜⬜

_____

- - - - - - - - - - -

_____

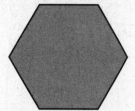

_____

- - - - - - - - -

———— **vertices**

DIRECTIONS **1.** Circle the set that shows an object shaped like a sphere above the object shaped like a cube. **2.** Count and tell how many. Write the number. **3.** How many vertices does the hexagon have? Write the number.

Name _____

Beside and Next To

COMMON CORE STANDARD—K.G.1
Identify and describe shapes (squares, circles, triangles, rectangles, hexagons, cubes, cones, cylinders, and spheres).

DIRECTIONS 1. Mark an X on the object shaped like a cylinder that is next to the object shaped like a sphere. Circle the object shaped like a cone that is beside the object shaped like a cube. Use the words *next to* and *beside* to name the position of other shapes.

Chapter 10

one hundred ninety-seven **P197**

Lesson Check (K.G.1)

Spiral Review (K.CC.3, K.G.2)

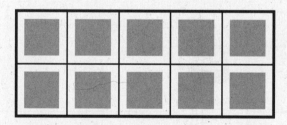

_____

_ _ _ _ _ _ _ _ _ _ _

_____

DIRECTIONS I. Circle the set that shows an object shaped like a cube beside the object shaped like a cone. **2.** Which shape is a hexagon? Color the hexagon. **3.** How many tiles are there? Write the number.

In Front Of and Behind

COMMON CORE STANDARD—K.G.1
Identify and describe shapes (squares, circles, triangles, rectangles, hexagons, cubes, cones, cylinders, and spheres).

DIRECTIONS **I.** Mark an X on the object shaped like a cylinder that is behind the object shaped like a cone. Draw a circle around the object shaped like a cylinder that is in front of the object shaped like a cube. Use the words *in front of* and *behind* to name the position of other shapes.

Chapter 10

Lesson Check (K.G.1)

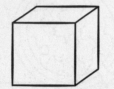 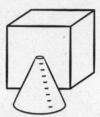

Spiral Review (K.OA.1, K.G.2)

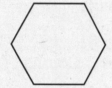

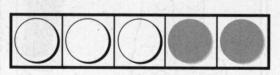

_____   _____

_ _ _ _   _ _ _ _

_____ **and** _____

DIRECTIONS 1. Circle the set that shows an object shaped like a cone in front of the object shaped like a cube. **2.** Which shape is a triangle? Color the triangle. **3.** How many of each color counter? Write the numbers.

P200 two hundred

School-Home Letter

Dear Family,

My class started Chapter 11 this week. In this chapter, I will learn how comparing objects can help me measure them.

Love, _____

Vocabulary

longer having a greater length

heavier having a greater weight

Home Activity

Find two different-sized books. Ask your child to show you how to compare their lengths, heights, and weights.

Literature

Look for these books at the library. Each book will give you ideas about how to enrich and encourage your child's measurement skills.

How Long or How Wide?: A Measuring Guide by Brian P. Cleary. Millbrook Press, 2007.

Measurement (Beginning Skills) by Amy Decastro. Teacher Created Resources, 2004.

Carta
para la casa

Querida familia:

Mi clase comenzó el Capítulo 11 esta semana. En este capítulo, aprenderé cómo comparar objetos puede ayudarme a medirlos.

Con cariño, _____

Vocabulario

más largo que que tiene mayor longitud

más pesado que tiene más peso

Actividad para la casa

Busque 2 libros de diferentes tamaños. Pídale a su hijo que le muestre cómo comparar la longitud, la altura y el peso.

Literatura

Busque estos libros en la biblioteca. Cada libro le dará ideas para enriquecer y alentar las destrezas de medición de su hijo.

How Long or How Wide?: A Measuring Guide por Brian P. Cleary. Millbrook Press, 2007.

Measurement (Beginning Skills) por Amy Decastro. Teacher Created Resources, 2004.

Compare Lengths

COMMON CORE STANDARD—K.MD.2
Describe and compare measurable attributes.

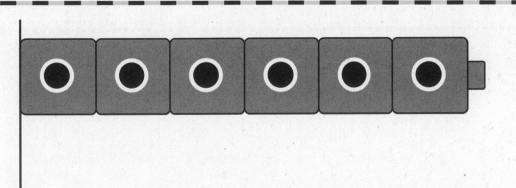

DIRECTIONS **1.** Make a cube train that is longer than the cube train shown. Draw and color the cube train. **2.** Make a cube train that is shorter than the cube train shown. Draw and color the cube train. **3.** Make a cube train that is about the same length as the cube train shown. Draw and color the cube train.

Lesson Check (K.MD.2)

 1

Spiral Review (K.G.2, K.G.4)

 2

3

DIRECTIONS 1. Make a cube train that is shorter than the cube train shown. Draw and color the cube train. 2. Which shape is a sphere? Mark an X on the shape. 3. Look at the shape. Draw a shape that is alike in some way. Tell how the two shapes are alike.

Name _____

Compare Heights

COMMON CORE STANDARD—K.MD.2
Describe and compare measurable attributes.

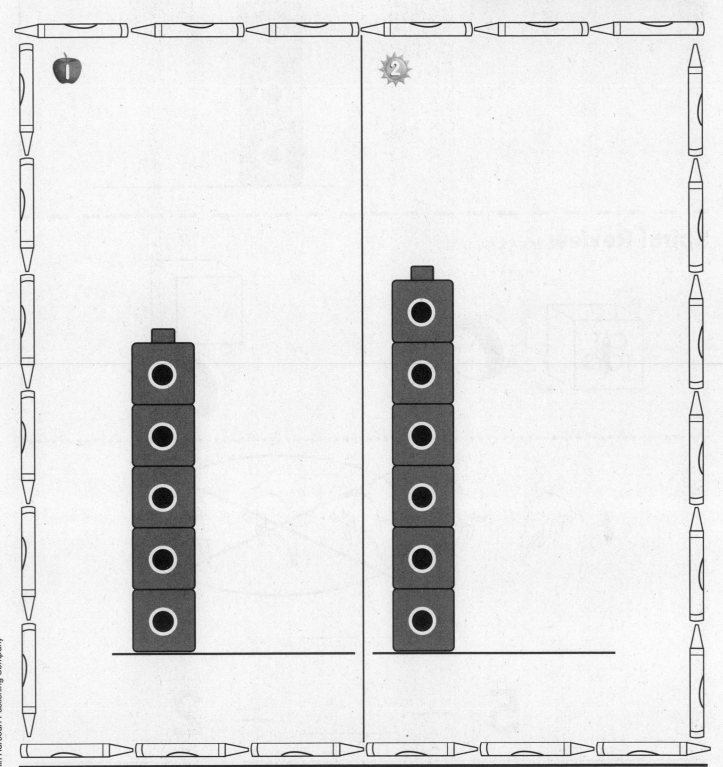

DIRECTIONS 1. Make a cube tower that is taller than the cube tower shown. Draw and color the cube tower. **2.** Make a cube tower that is shorter than the cube tower shown. Draw and color the cube tower.

Chapter 11

Lesson Check (K.MD.2)

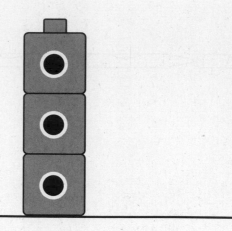

Spiral Review (K.OA.5, K.G.1)

 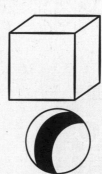

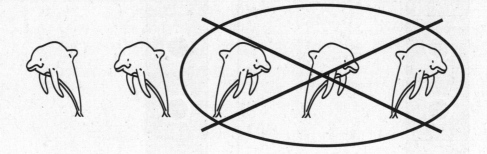

_____

- - - - -

$5 - \underline{} = 2$

DIRECTIONS 1. Make a cube tower that is shorter than the cube tower shown. Draw and color the cube tower. 2. Circle the set that shows an object shaped like a sphere below the object shaped like a cube. 3. How many are being taken from the set? Write the number.

P206 two hundred six

Name _____

Problem Solving • Direct Comparison

COMMON CORE STANDARD—K.MD.2
Describe and compare measurable attributes.

DIRECTIONS **1.** Find two small classroom objects. Place one end of each object on the line. Compare the lengths. Draw the objects. Say *longer than*, *shorter than*, or *about the same length* to describe the lengths. Circle the longer object. **2.** Find two small classroom objects. Place one end of each object on the line. Compare the heights. Draw the objects. Say *taller than*, *shorter than*, or *about the same height* to describe the heights. Circle the shorter object.

Chapter 11

Lesson Check (K.MD.2)

Spiral Review (K.0A.2, K.G.4)

_____ vertices

DIRECTIONS 1. Find two pencils. Place one end of each pencil on the line. Compare the lengths. Draw the pencils. Say *longer than, shorter than,* or *about the same length* to describe the lengths. Circle the shorter pencil. **2.** How many vertices does the rectangle have? Write the number. **3.** Complete the subtraction sentence to show the numbers that match the cube train.

Name _____

Compare Weights

COMMON CORE STANDARD—K.MD.2
Describe and compare measurable attributes.

 left    **right**

 1  |

 2 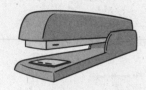 |

 3  |

 4  |

DIRECTIONS   Find the first object in the row, and hold it in your left hand. Find the rest of the objects in the row, and hold each object in your right hand.   **1–2.** Circle the object that is lighter than the object in your left hand.   **3–4.** Circle the object that is heavier than the object in your left hand.

Lesson Check (K.MD.2)

1

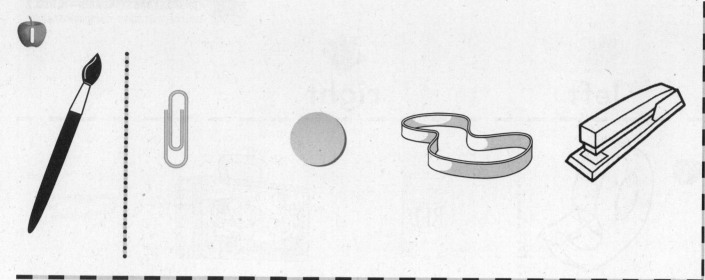

Spiral Review (K.CC.6, K.G.3)

2

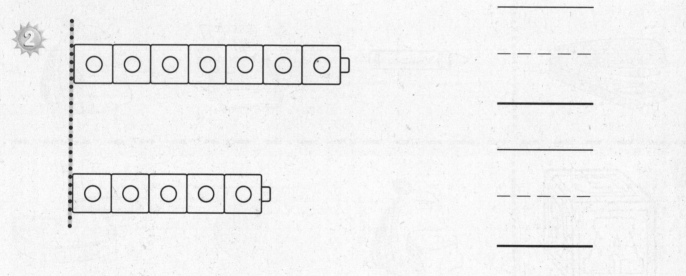

_____

- - - - -

_____

- - - - -

_____

3

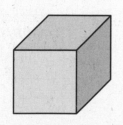  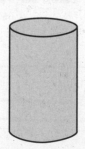

DIRECTIONS **1.** Find a paintbrush. Hold it in your left hand. Find the rest of the objects in the row, and hold each object in your right hand. Circle the object that is heavier than the paintbrush. **2.** Count the cubes. Write how many. Circle the number that is less. **3.** Which is a two-dimensional or flat shape? Mark an X on the shape.

Length, Height, and Weight

COMMON CORE STANDARD—K.MD.1
Describe and compare measurable attributes.

DIRECTIONS 1–4. Use red to trace the line that shows how to measure the length. Use blue to trace the line that shows how to measure the height. Talk about another way to measure the object.

© Houghton Mifflin Harcourt Publishing Company

Lesson Check (K.MD.1)

Spiral Review (K.NBT.1, K.G.2)

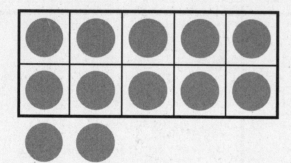

DIRECTIONS **1.** Use red to trace the line that shows how to measure the length. Use blue to trace the line that shows how to measure the height. **2.** Count and tell how many. Write the number. **3.** Which shape is a rectangle? Color the rectangle.

School-Home
Letter

Dear Family,

My class started Chapter 12 this week. In this chapter, I will learn how sorting can help me display information.

Love, _____

Vocabulary

category

Small

Large

These shapes are sorted and classified into two categories. One category is *small*, and one category is *large*.

Home Activity

Have some fun in the kitchen as your child shows you all about sorting and classifying. Begin by collecting a handful of silverware. Have your child sort and classify it into groups by type of utensil.

Literature

Look for these books at the library. Your child will continue learning while enjoying these great books.

Sorting
by Henry Arthur Pluckrose.
Children's Press, 1995.

Grandma's Button Box
by Linda Williams Aber.
Kane Press, 2002.

Carta
para la casa

Querida familia:

Mi clase comenzó el Capítulo 12 esta semana. En este capítulo, aprenderé cómo clasi car puede ayudarme a mostrar información.

Con cariño, _____

Vocabulario

categoría

grandes

pequeños

Estos figuras se clasifican en dos categorías. Una categoría es *pequeños* y la otra categoría es *grandes*.

Actividad para la casa

Diviértanse en la cocina mientras su hijo le muestra todo sobre cómo clasificar. Comience por tomar algunos cubiertos. Pídale a su hijo que los clasifique en grupos según el tipo de utensilio.

Literatura

Busque este libro en la biblioteca. Su hijo seguirá aprendiendo mientras disfruta de este excelente libro.

Sorting
por Henry Arthur Pluckrose.
Children's Press, 1995.

Grandma's Button Box
por Linda Williams Aber.
Kane Press, 2002

Algebra • Classify and Count by Color

COMMON CORE STANDARD—K.MD.3
Classify objects and count the number of objects in each category.

yellow	red

3    yellow    red   _____

_____

_____

DIRECTIONS   1. Place a yellow square, red triangle, red rectangle, yellow square, and red triangle at the top of the page as shown. Sort and classify the shapes by the category of color. Draw and color the shapes in each category.   2. Look at the categories in Exercise 1. Count how many in each category. Circle the category that has 3 shapes. Write the number.

Lesson Check (K.MD.3)

_____

- - - - - - - - - - - - - -

_____

Spiral Review (K.CC.3, K.G.4)

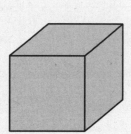  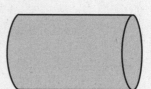

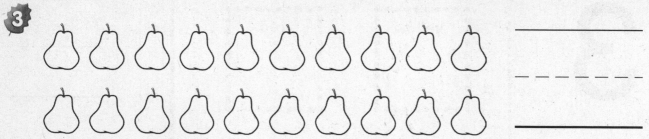

DIRECTIONS **1.** Look at the set of shapes. Which shape belongs in the same category? Draw that shape in the box and color it. How many shapes are in the category now? Write the number. **2.** Which shape does not stack? Mark an X on the shape. **3.** Count and tell how many pieces of fruit. Write the number.

Algebra • Classify and Count by Shape

1

triangle	circle

2

2

triangle	circle

_____

DIRECTIONS **1.** Place a green triangle, blue circle, red triangle and blue circle at the top of the page as shown. Sort and classify the shapes by the category of shape. Draw and color the shapes in each category. **2.** Look at the categories in Exercise 1. Count how many in each category. Circle the categories that have two shapes. Write the number.

Lesson Check (K.MD.3)

_____

_ _ _ _ _ _ _

_____

Spiral Review (K.OA.3, K.MD.2)

5

DIRECTIONS 1. Look at the set of shapes. Which shape belongs in the same category? Draw that shape in the oval. How many shapes are in the category now? Write the number. 2. Find two crayons. Place one end of each crayon on the line. Compare the lengths. Draw the crayons. Say *longer than*, *shorter than*, or *about the same length* to describe the lengths. Circle the longer crayon. 3. Complete the addition sentence to show the numbers that match the cube train.

Algebra • Classify and Count by Size

COMMON CORE STANDARD—K.MD.3
Classify objects and count the number of objects in each category.

small	big

2

small   big   _____
___ ___ ___
_____

DIRECTIONS 1. Place a yellow square, blue circle, red rectangle, and blue rectangle at the top of the page as shown. Sort and classify the shapes by the category of size. Draw and color the shapes in each category. **2.** Look at the categories in Exercise 1. Count how many in each category. Circle the category that has one per category. Write the number.

Lesson Check (K.MD.3)

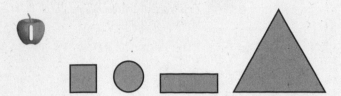

small	big

Spiral Review (K.OA.5, K.G.2)

2

_____

- - - - - - - -

_____

3

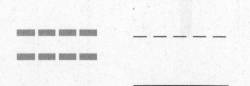

DIRECTIONS   1. Sort and classify the shapes by the category of size. Draw the shapes in each category.   **2.** How many flat surfaces does the cylinder have? Write the number.   **3.** Sarah makes a five-cube train. She takes the cube train apart to show how many cubes are gray. Trace and write to show the subtraction sentence for Sarah's cube train.

Name _____

Make a Concrete Graph

COMMON CORE STANDARD—K.MD.3
Classify objects and count the number of
objects in each category.

 1

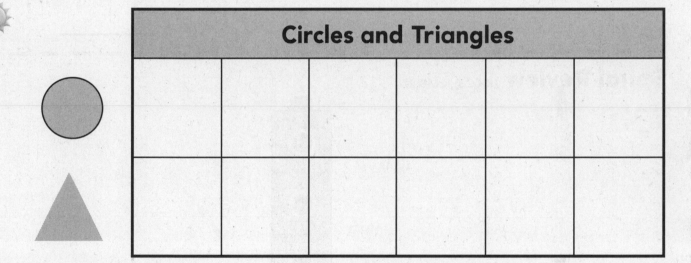

2

Circles and Triangles					

3

DIRECTIONS **1.** Place a handful of green circles and triangles on the workspace. Sort and classify the shapes by category. **2.** Move the shapes to the graph. Draw and color the shapes. **3.** Write how many of each shape.

© Houghton Mifflin Harcourt Publishing Company

Lesson Check (K.MD.3)

Triangles and Squares

_____   _____

 - - - - - - - - -   ■   - - - - - - - - -

_____   _____

Spiral Review (K.CC.3, K.MD.2)

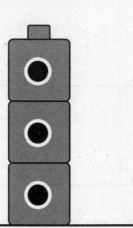

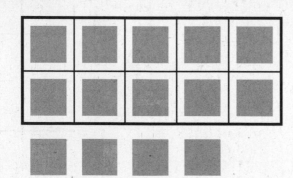

_____

- - - - - - - - -

_____

DIRECTIONS **1.** Look at the shapes. Draw and color the shapes in the graph. Write how many of each shape. **2.** Make a cube train that is about the same height as the cube train shown. Draw and color the cube train. **3.** How many tiles are there? Write the number.

Name _____

Read a Graph

COMMON CORE STANDARD—K.MD.3
Classify objects and count the number of objects in each category.

Counter Colors

🍎 **1**

2

DIRECTIONS **1.** Color the counters to show the categories. R is for red, and Y is for yellow. How many counters are in each category? Write the numbers. **2.** Circle the category that has more counters on the graph.

© Houghton Mifflin Harcourt Publishing Company

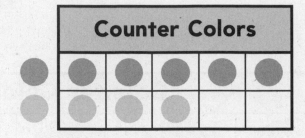

8

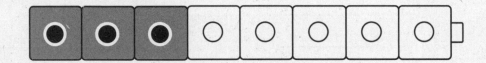

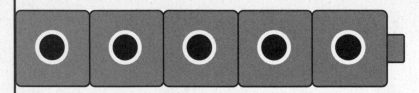

DIRECTIONS 1. How many counters are in each category? Write the numbers. Circle the category that has more counters. **2.** Complete the addition sentence to show the numbers that match the cube train. **3.** Make a cube train that is about the same length as the cube train shown. Draw and color the cube train.

Name _____

Add One

 +  =

2 + _____ = _____

3 + _____ = _____

© Houghton Mifflin Harcourt Publishing Company

DIRECTIONS 1. Place cubes as shown above the numbers.
Trace the cubes. Trace to complete the addition sentence.
2–3. Use cubes to show the number. Draw the cubes.
Show and draw one more cube. Complete the addition sentence.

Getting Ready for Grade 1

4

$$5 + \_\_\_\_\_ = \_\_\_\_\_$$

5

$$6 + \_\_\_\_\_ = \_\_\_\_\_$$

6

$$7 + \_\_\_\_\_ = \_\_\_\_\_$$

DIRECTIONS   4–6. Use cubes to show the number. Draw the cubes. Show and draw one more cube. Complete the addition sentence.

HOME ACTIVITY • Show your child a set of one to nine pennies. Have him or her use pennies to show how to add one to the set. Then have him or her tell how many in all.

Add Two

1 + 2 = 3

___ + ___ = ___

___ + ___ = ___

DIRECTIONS 1. Count how many shells in the first group. Trace the two shells. Trace to complete the addition sentence. **2–3.** Count how many shells. Write the number. Draw two more shells. Complete the addition sentence.

Getting Ready for Grade 1

two hundred twenty-seven **P227**

_____

- - - - - - -   +   - - - - - - -   =   - - - - - - -

_____

_____

- - - - - - -   +   - - - - - - -   =   - - - - - - -

_____

_____

- - - - - - -   +   - - - - - - -   =   - - - - - - -

_____

DIRECTIONS 4–6. Count how many shells there are. Write the number. Draw two more shells. Complete the addition sentence.

HOME ACTIVITY • Draw objects in a column beginning with a set of 1 to a set of 8. Have your child draw two more objects beside each set, and write how many in all.

P228 two hundred twenty-eight

Name _____

Add on a Ten Frame

red	red	red	red	red
yellow	yellow	yellow	yellow	yellow

$$5 + 5 = 10$$

---

②

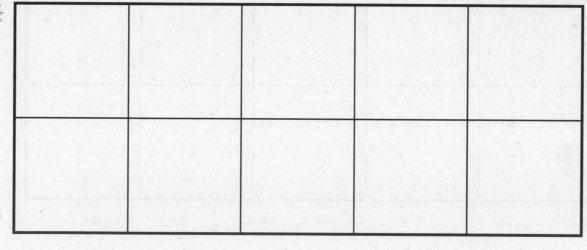

_____ _____ _____ _____
         +   =
_____   _____   _____

DIRECTIONS I. Place counters on the ten frame as shown. Trace the addition sentence. 2. Place some counters red side up on the ten frame. Add more counters yellow side up to fill the ten frame. Complete the addition sentence.

Getting Ready for Grade I two hundred twenty-nine **P229**

3

_____ + _____ = _____

4

_____ + _____ = _____

HOME ACTIVITY • Give your child some household objects, such as two different kinds of buttons. Have your child arrange the buttons to show different ways to make 10, such as 6 red buttons and 4 blue buttons. Write the addition sentence.

© Houghton Mifflin Harcourt Publishing Company

Part-Part-Whole

① | **Whole**
2

Part | **Part**

2 | **0**

 ② | **Whole**
3

Part | **Part**

DIRECTIONS 1–2. How many cubes are there in all? Place that many cubes in the workspace. Show the parts that make the whole. Complete the chart to show all the parts that make the whole.

Getting Ready for Grade 1

two hundred thirty-one **P231**

Whole
4

Part	Part
_____	_____
- - - -	- - - -
_____	_____
_____	_____
- - - -	- - - -
_____	_____
_____	_____
- - - -	- - - -
_____	_____
_____	_____
- - - -	- - - -
_____	_____
_____	_____
- - - -	- - - -
_____	_____

Whole
5

Part	Part
_____	_____
- - - -	- - - -
_____	_____
_____	_____
- - - -	- - - -
_____	_____
_____	_____
- - - -	- - - -
_____	_____
_____	_____
- - - -	- - - -
_____	_____
_____	_____
- - - -	- - - -
_____	_____

DIRECTIONS **3–4.** How many cubes are there in all? Complete the chart to show all the parts that make the whole.

HOME ACTIVITY • Have your child use buttons or macaroni pieces to show the different parts that make the whole set of 8 (e.g. 7 and 1, 6 and 2, 5 and 3, 4 and 4.)

Name _____

Equal Sets

 1

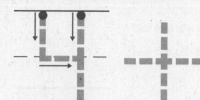 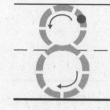

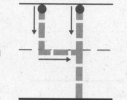

 2

_____   _____   _____

 3

_____   _____   _____

_____   _____   _____

DIRECTIONS   Count the cubes. Use cubes to make an equal set.
1. Trace the cubes. Trace the addition sentence.   **2–3.** Draw the
cubes. Write and trace to complete the addition sentence.

Getting Ready for Grade 1

4

_____ + _____ = _____

5

_____ + _____ = _____

6

_____ + _____ = _____

DIRECTIONS 4–6. Count the cubes. Use cubes to make an equal set. Draw the cubes. Write and trace to complete the addition sentence.

HOME ACTIVITY • Have your child show equal sets by holding up an equal number of fingers on each hand. Then have your child say the addition sentence.

P234 two hundred thirty-four

© Houghton Mifflin Harcourt Publishing Company

Name _____

Concepts and Skills

 1

4 + ___ ___ === ___

2

<table>
<tr><td></td><td></td><td></td><td></td><td></td></tr>
<tr><td></td><td></td><td></td><td></td><td></td></tr>
</table>

___ + ___ === ___

DIRECTIONS 1. Use cubes to show the number. Draw the cubes. Show and draw one more cube. Complete the addition sentence.
2. Place some counters red side up on the ten frame. Add more counters yellow side up to fill the ten frame. Complete the addition sentence.

Whole

2

Part	Part
2	0

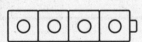

4

DIRECTIONS **3.** How many cubes are there in all? Place that many cubes in the workspace. Show the different parts that make the whole. Complete the chart to show all the parts that make the whole. **4.** Count the cubes. Use cubes to make an equal set. Draw the cubes. Trace and write to complete the addition sentence.

Name _____

Related Addition Equations

1

$1 + 3 = 2 + 2$

2

___ + ___ = ___ + ___

3

___ + ___ = ___ + ___

DIRECTIONS Look at the cube trains. **1.** Trace to complete the equation. **2–3.** Trace and write to complete the equation.

Getting Ready for Grade 1

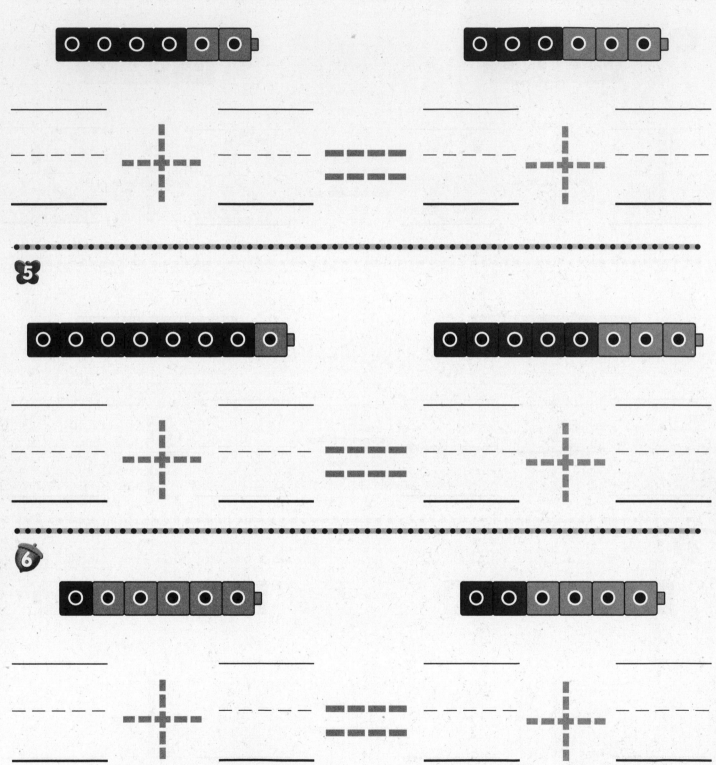

4.

_____ + _____ = _____ + _____

5.

_____ + _____ = _____ + _____

6.

_____ + _____ = _____ + _____

DIRECTIONS 4–6. Look at the cube trains. Trace and write to complete the equation.

HOME ACTIVITY • Place 5 pennies on the table. Have your child group the pennies in different ways, such as 3 + 2 or 4 + 1.

Name _____

Subtract One

10 -- 1 == 9

9 -- ___ ___ == ___ ___ ___

8 -- ___ ___ == ___ ___ ___

DIRECTIONS 1. Place cubes on the ones shown. Trace the cubes. Trace the circle and X on the cube being taken away. Trace to complete the subtraction sentence. **2–3.** Use cubes to show the number. Draw the cubes. Take away one cube. Circle the cube that you took away and mark an X on it. Complete the subtraction sentence.

Getting Ready for Grade 1

two hundred thirty-nine **P239**

7 ----

5

6 ----

6

5 ----

DIRECTIONS 4–6. Use cubes to show the number. Draw the cubes. Take away one cube. Circle the cube that you took away and mark an X on it. Complete the subtraction sentence.

HOME ACTIVITY • Ask your child to use toys to demonstrate and describe the number pattern in the subtraction sentences on this page.

Name _____

Subtract Two

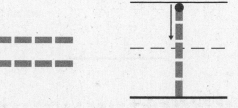

DIRECTIONS 1. Count how many boats there are in all. Trace the circle and the X that shows the boats that sail away. Trace to complete the subtraction sentence. **2–3.** Count how many boats there are in all. Write the number. Two boats sail away. Circle the boats that sail away. Mark an X on them. Complete the subtraction sentence.

Getting Ready for Grade 1

4

_____   _____   _____

_ _ _ _   ▬ ▬ ▬ ▬   _ _ _ _   ▬▬ ▬ ▬   _ _ _ _
                                      ▬ ▬ ▬

_____   _____   _____

5

_____   _____   _____

_ _ _ _   ▬ ▬ ▬ ▬   _ _ _ _   ▬ ▬ ▬ ▬   _ _ _ _
                                      ▬ ▬ ▬ ▬

_____   _____   _____

6

_____   _____   _____

_ _ _ _   ▬ ▬ ▬   _ _ _ _   ▬ ▬ ▬ ▬   _ _ _ _
                                    ▬ ▬ ▬ ▬

_____   _____   _____

DIRECTIONS 4–6. Count how many boats there are in all. Write the number. Two boats sail away. Circle the boats that sail away. Mark an X on them. Complete the subtraction sentence.

HOME ACTIVITY • Give your child five buttons. Have your child take away two buttons and tell how many are left.

Name _____

Subtract on a Ten Frame

| red | red | red | red | red |
| red | red | red | red | red |

10 - 4 = 6

- -

2

| | | | | |
| | | | | |

_____   _____   _____

- -

_____   _____   _____

DIRECTIONS 1. Place 10 counters as shown on the ten frame. Take away 4 counters. Trace the circle around the set of counters that you took away. Trace the X on that set. Trace the subtraction sentence. 2. Place 10 counters on the ten frame. Draw the counters. Take away some counters. Circle the set of counters that you took away. Mark an X on that set. Complete the subtraction sentence.

Getting Ready for Grade 1   two hundred forty-three **P243**

3

_____   _____   _____

- - - - - - - ▬▬▬▬   - - - - - - - ▬▬▬▬
                                                ▬▬▬▬

_____   _____   _____

• •

4

_____   _____   _____

- - - - - - - ▬▬▬▬   - - - - - - - ▬▬▬▬
                                                ▬▬▬▬

_____   _____   _____

• •

DIRECTIONS   3–4. Place 10 counters on the ten frame. Draw the counters. Take away some counters. Circle the set of counters that you took away. Mark an X on that set. Complete the subtraction sentence.

HOME ACTIVITY • Give your child ten household objects, such as buttons. Have your child take some of the objects away. Then have him or her tell the subtraction sentence.

Algebra: Missing Part

Whole	
2	
Part	Part
2	0
1	___
0	___

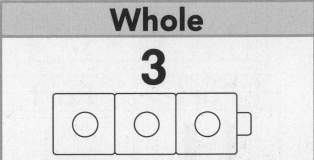

Whole	
3	
Part	Part
3	___
2	___
1	___
0	___

DIRECTIONS 1–2. How many cubes are there in all? Complete the chart to show the missing part that makes the whole.

Getting Ready for Grade 1

3

Whole 4	
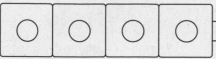	
Part	**Part**
4	___
3	___
2	___
1	___
0	___

4

Whole 5	
Part	**Part**
5	___
4	___
3	___
2	___
1	___
0	___

DIRECTIONS 3–4. How many cubes are there in all? Complete the chart to show the missing part that makes the whole.

HOME ACTIVITY • Place 8 spoons on the table. Cover 3 of the spoons. Tell your child that you started with 8 spoons. Ask him or her to tell you how many spoons are covered.

Name _____

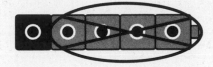

Related Subtraction Equations

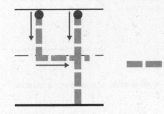 

 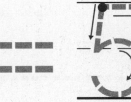 

$$4 - 3 = 5 - 4$$

_____ _____ _____

___ - ___ = ___ - ___

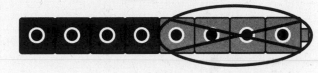

❸

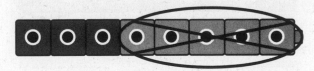

___ - ___ = ___ - ___

DIRECTIONS Look at the cube trains. **1.** Trace to complete the equation.
2–3. Trace and write to complete the equation.

Getting Ready for Grade 1

4

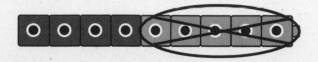

_____ _____   _____

- - - -   ▭▭▭   - - - -   ▭▭▭▭   - - - -   ▭▭▭   - - - -
                            ▭▭▭▭

_____   _____   _____ _____

• •

5

_____ _____   _____ _____

- - - -   ▭▭▭   - - - -   ▭▭▭   - - - -   ▭▭▭   - - - -
                            ▭▭▭

_____   _____   _____ _____

• •

6

_____   _____   _____

- - - -   ▭▭▭   - - - -   ▭▭▭▭   - - - -   ▭▭▭   - - - -
                            ▭▭▭▭

_____   _____   _____

• •

DIRECTIONS   4–6. Look at the cube trains. Trace and write to complete the equation.

HOME ACTIVITY • Say a subtraction fact with a difference of 2. Have your child say another subtraction fact with a difference of 2.

Related Addition and Subtraction Equations

$$3 + 3 = 8 - 2$$

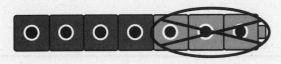 

DIRECTIONS Look at the cube trains. **1.** Trace to complete the equation.
2–3. Trace and write to complete the equation.

Getting Ready for Grade 1

two hundred forty-nine **P249**

4

_____ _____   _____ _____

----- --- -----   ===== ----- --+-- -----

_____ _____   _____ _____

5

_____ _____   _____ _____

----- --- -----   ===== ----- --+-- -----

_____ _____   _____ _____

6

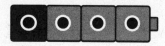

_____ _____   _____ _____

----- --+-- -----   ===== --- -----

_____ _____   _____ _____

HOME ACTIVITY • Say an addition fact with a sum of 5. Then ask your child to say a subtraction fact with a difference of 5.

Subtract to Compare

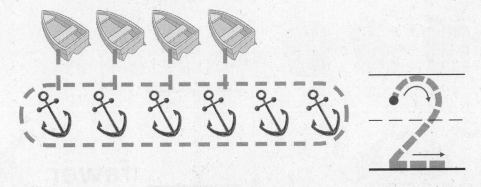

 more

2

_____

- - - - - - - - -

_____ **more**

3

_____

- - - - - - - - -

_____ **more**

DIRECTIONS **1.** Trace the lines to match the objects in the top row to the objects in the bottom row. Compare the sets. Trace the circle that shows the set with more objects. Trace the number. **2–3.** Draw lines to match the objects in the top row to the objects in the bottom row. Compare the sets. Circle the set that has more objects. Write how many more.

© Houghton Mifflin Harcourt Publishing Company

Getting Ready for Grade 1

4

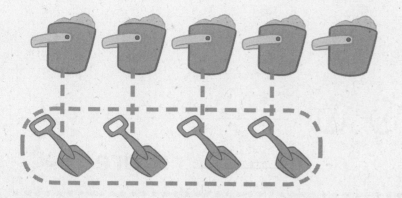

 fewer

5

_____

- - - - - - -

_____ fewer 🏰

6

_____

- - - - - - -

_____ fewer

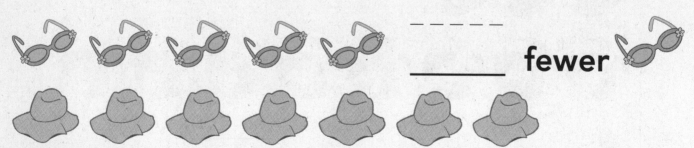

DIRECTIONS 4. Trace the lines to match the objects in the top row to the objects in the bottom row. Compare the sets. Trace the circle that shows the set with fewer objects. Trace the number. **5–6.** Draw lines to match the objects in the top row to the objects in the bottom row. Compare the sets. Circle the set that has fewer objects. Write how many fewer.

HOME ACTIVITY • Show your child a row of seven pennies and a row of three nickels. Have your child compare the sets, identify which has fewer coins, and tell how many fewer. Repeat with other sets of coins up to ten.

Name _____

 **Checkpoint**

2 __ __   __ __ __   ▬▬▬ __ __
                            ▬▬▬

__ __ __   __ __   ▬▬▬▬ __ __
                       ▬▬▬▬

DIRECTIONS 1. Use cubes to show the number. Draw the cubes. Take away one cube. Circle the cube that you took away and mark an X on it. Complete the subtraction sentence. **2.** Place 10 counters on the ten frame. Draw the counters. Take away some counters. Circle and mark an X on the counters that you took away. Complete the subtraction sentence.

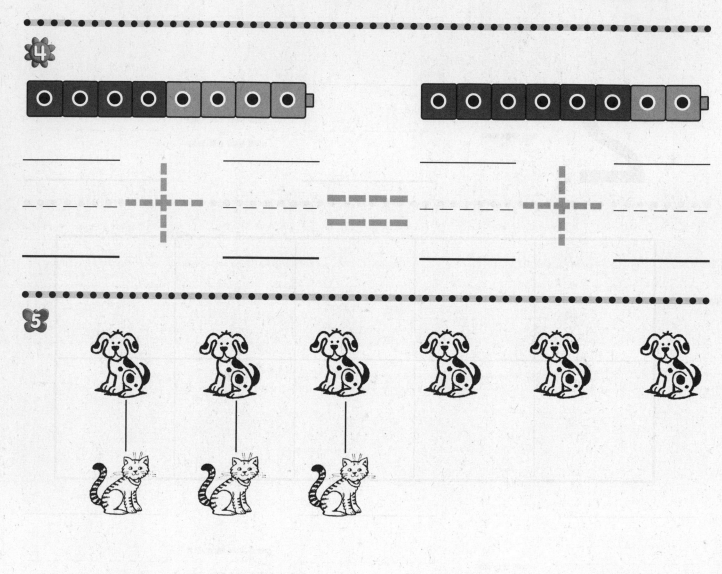

3.

_____ _____ _____ _____

- - - ▭▭▭ - - - ▭▭▭ - - -
                        ▭▭▭

_____   _____   _____

4.

- - - ╋ _____   ▭▭▭ - - - ╋ _____
                   ▭▭▭

_____   _____   _____

5.

| 2 | 3 | 4 | 5 |
| ○ | ○ | ○ | ○ |

DIRECTIONS **3.** Count and write how many boats in all. Two boats leave. Circle and mark an X on those boats. Complete the subtraction sentence. **4.** Look at the cube trains. Trace and write to complete the equation. **5.** Compare the sets. Mark under the number that shows how many more dogs are shown in the picture.

Name _____

Hands On: How Many Ones?

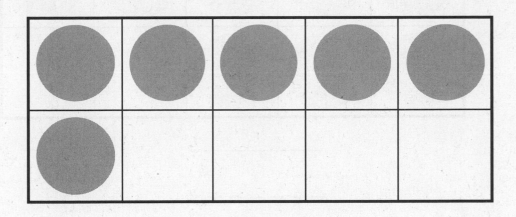

_____

- - - - - - - -

_____ ones

••

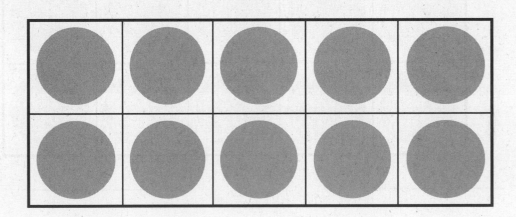

_____   _____

- - - - - - - -

_____ ones or _____ ten

••

DIRECTIONS Place counters on the ones shown. **1.** How many ones
are there? Write the number. **2.** How many ones are there? Write the
number. How many tens is that? Write the number.

3

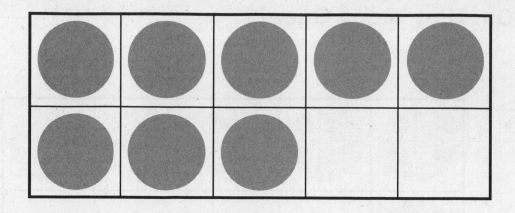

_____

_ _ _ _ _ _ _ _

_____ **ones**

4

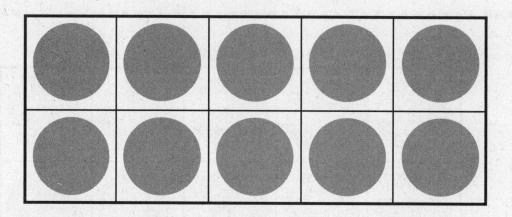

_____   _____

_ _ _ _ _ _ _   _ _ _ _ _ _ _

_____ **ones   or   _____ ten**

DIRECTIONS Place counters on the ones shown. **3.** How many ones are there? Write the number. **4.** How many ones are there? How many tens is that? Write the number.

HOME ACTIVITY • Place 10 small items on a table. Ask your child to count and write how many ones that is. Then ask him or her to write how many tens that is.

Name _____

Read and Write Numbers 20 to 30

 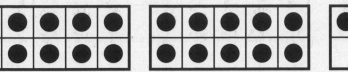

_____
_____

  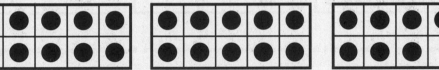 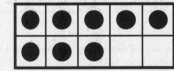

_____

 ③

_____

④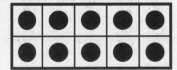

_____

⑤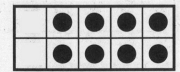

_____

DIRECTIONS How many counters are there? 1. Trace the number. 2–5. Write the number.

Getting Ready for Grade 1

6

7

8

9

10

DIRECTIONS 6–10. How many counters are there? Write the number.

HOME ACTIVITY • Give your child 20 to 30 paper clips. Have your child count the paper clips and write how many.

Name _____

Read and Write Numbers 30 to 40

 1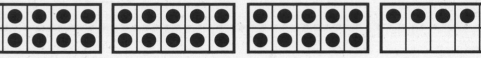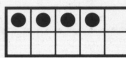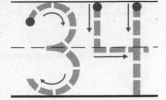

 2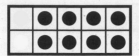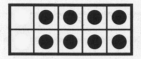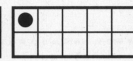

3

 4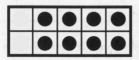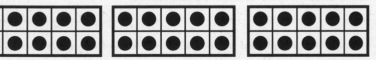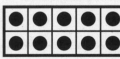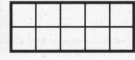

5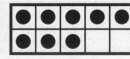

   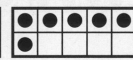

DIRECTIONS How many counters are there? 1. Trace the number. 2–5. Write the number.

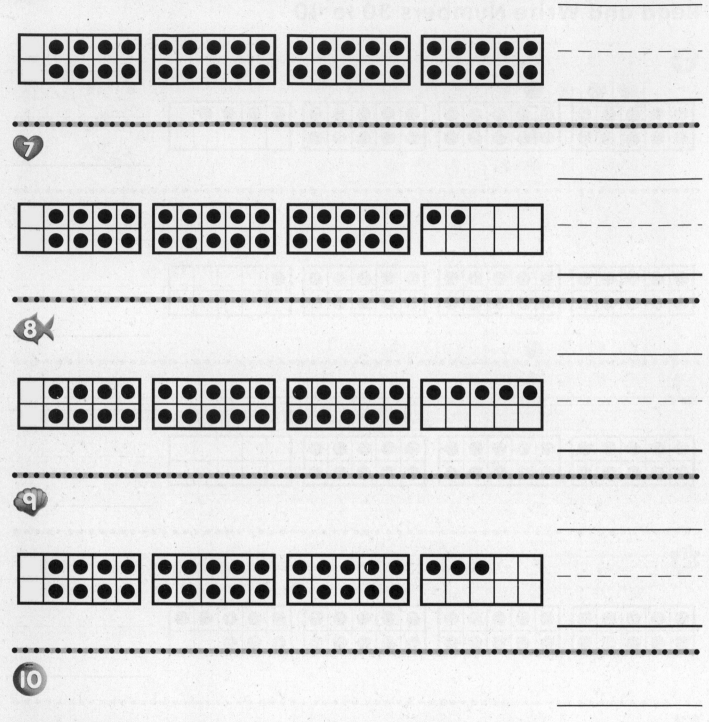

DIRECTIONS 6–10. How many counters are there? Write the number.

HOME ACTIVITY • Have your child count out cereal pieces for different numbers from 30 to 40.

P260 two hundred sixty

© Houghton Mifflin Harcourt Publishing Company

Read and Write Numbers 40 to 50

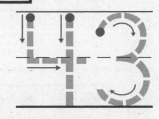

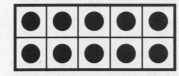
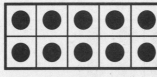

_____

_ _ _ _ _ _ _ _ _

_____

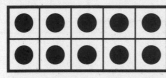
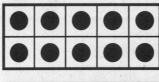

_____

_ _ _ _ _ _ _ _ _

_____

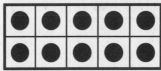

_____

_ _ _ _ _ _ _ _ _

_____

DIRECTIONS How many counters are there?
1. Trace the number. 2–4. Write the number.

Getting Ready for Grade 1

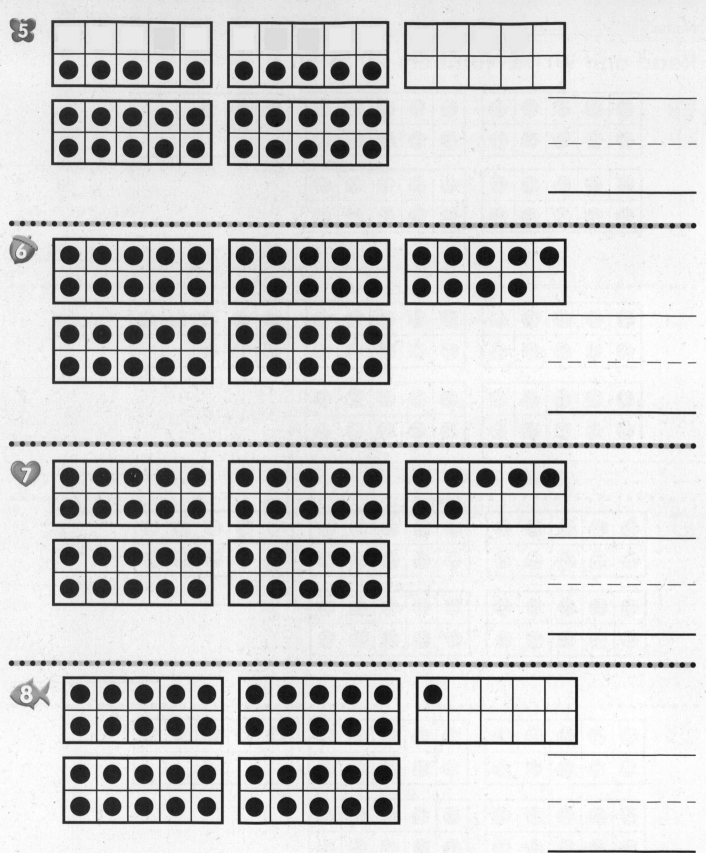

5

6

7

8

DIRECTIONS 5–8. How many counters are there? Write the number.

HOME ACTIVITY • Help your child count four sets of ten cereal pieces each. Then have him or her tell how many cereal pieces there are.

Name _____

 # ✓ Checkpoint

1

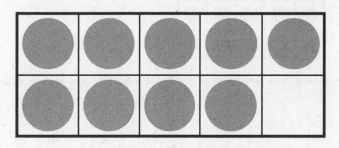

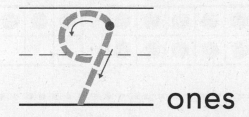 ones

 2

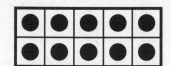 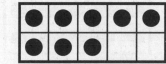

_ _ _ _ _ _ _ _ _ _
_____

 3

_ _ _ _ _ _ _ _ _ _
_____

DIRECTIONS **1.** How many ones are there? Write the number. **2–3.** How many counters are there? Write the number.

Getting Ready for Grade 1

two hundred sixty-three **P263**

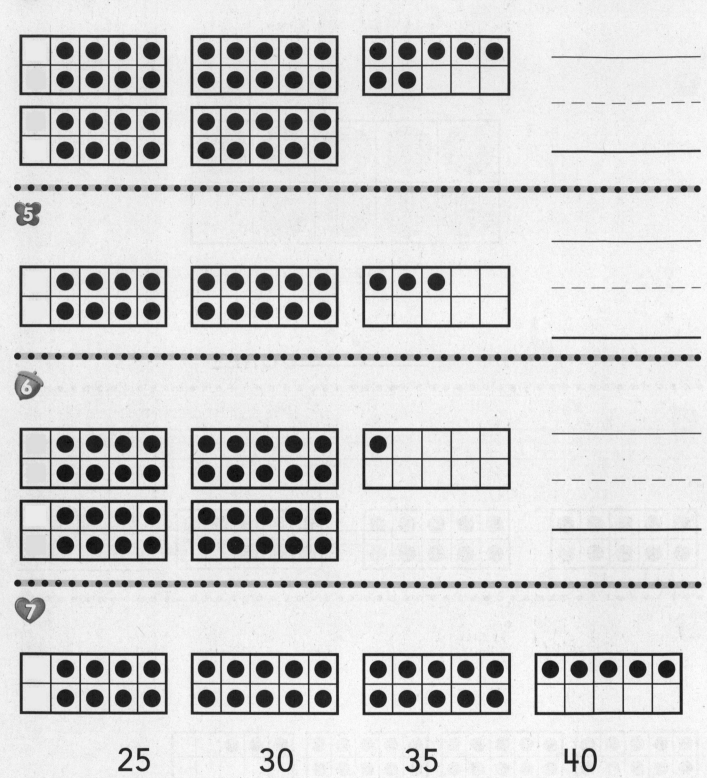

4

5

6

7

25   30   35   40
○   ○   ○   ○

DIRECTIONS   4–6. How many counters are there? Write the number.
7. How many counters are shown? Mark under the number of counters.

Numbers on a Clock

DIRECTIONS   **I.** Trace 12 at the top of the clock.   Write the numbers I to 6 in order on the clock.

Getting Ready for Grade I

two hundred sixty-five **P265**

DIRECTIONS 2. Find 6 on the the
clock. Write the numbers 7 to 12 in order
on the clock.

HOME ACTIVITY • Have your child point to
and name the numbers on an analog clock.

Name _____

Use an Analog Clock

 **o'clock**

_____

__ __ __ __ __

_____ **o'clock**

_____

__ __ __ __ __

_____ **o'clock**

_____

__ __ __ __ __

_____ **o'clock**

DIRECTIONS 1. About what time does the clock show?
Trace the number. **2–4.** About what time does the clock show?
Write the number.

Getting Ready for Grade 1

before 6 o'clock   about 6 o'clock   after 6 o'clock

5

before 2 o'clock

about 2 o'clock

after 2 o'clock

6

before 7 o'clock

about 7 o'clock

after 7 o'clock

7

before 11 o'clock

about 11 o'clock

after 11 o'clock

DIRECTIONS 5–7. Circle the time shown on the clock.

 HOME ACTIVITY • Look at or draw a simple clock. Ask your child questions such as: *Where does the hour hand go to show about 8 o'clock? About 1 o'clock? About 4 o'clock?*

Name _____

Use a Digital Clock

 1

 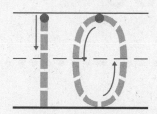 o'clock

 2

 _____ o'clock

 3

 _____ o'clock

 4

 _____ o'clock

DIRECTIONS **1.** Trace the hour number on the digital clock. Trace to show another way to write that time. **2–4.** Trace the hour number on the digital clock. Show another way to write that time.

5

6:00

_____
- - - - - - -
_____ **o'clock**

6

2:00

_____
- - - - - - -
_____ **o'clock**

7

11:00

_____
- - - - - - -
_____ **o'clock**

8

8:00

_____
- - - - - - -
_____ **o'clock**

DIRECTIONS 5–8. Trace the hour number on the digital clock. Show another way to write that time.

HOME ACTIVITY • Ask your child to explain or draw what a digital clock looks like at 3:00.

✓ Checkpoint

 1

• •

 2

before 9 o'clock

about 9 o'clock

after 9 o'clock

DIRECTIONS 1. Write the missing numbers on the clock.
2. Circle the time shown on the clock.

Getting Ready for Grade 1

two hundred seventy-one **P271**

3

$\underline{7}$:00

_____

- - - - - - -

_____ o'clock

4

5

2   6   7   8
○   ○   ○   ○

DIRECTIONS **3.** Trace the hour number on the clock. Show another way to write that time. **4.** Write the missing numbers on the clock. **5.** Mark under the number that shows about what time is on the clock.